ADULT ADOPTEE ANTHOLOGY

Flip The Script

EDITED AND COMPILED BY

ROSITA GONZÁLEZ, AMANDA TRANSUE-WOOLSTON, LSW, DIANE RENÉ CHRISTIAN

The An-Ya Project

An-Ya and Her Diary: The Novel (April, 2012)

An-Ya and Her Diary: Reader & Parent Guide (April, 2013)

Perpetual Child: Adult Adoptee Anthology (Winter, 2013)

Dear Wonderful You, Letters to Adopted & Fostered Youth (2014)

Flip the Script: Adult Adoptee Anthology (2015)

For more information on the An-Ya Project visit:
www.anyadiary.com

The Souls Of Clear Folk

How do you see
The souls of those whose bodies are invisible?
Is not to be human
To also be indivisible?
When they say there's no shame,
That we're all the same
There's nothing more dismissible.
In my journey to be whole,
I find myself sitting in one.

Stuck in a valley
Of broken vessels and wasted dreams
The scent of stale breath reeks of shattered memories
Our tattered stories prying through the cracks of a rotten egg
Can you hear the sounds of subversion?
We are the leathered skin of our grandmother's smile
Teaming with wisdom and unfettered authority
We are the native daughters
Searching for a place to call our own

By Stephen David Lukeson

Table of Contents

Dedication 11

Foreword 13

JOE SOLL 조 살, LCSW - Art & Essay 16

KEVIN MINH ALLEN - Essay 20

SUSAN ITO - Essay 22

ADEL KSK - Art 26

APRIL DINWOODIE - Essay 30

LUCY CHAU LAI-TUEN - Poetry & Mixed Media 32

KATIE HAE LEO - Essay 36

LAURA COTTER - Essay 40

MELISSA DAE SOOK KIM - Art 42

MEGGIN NAM HOLTZ - Poetry 44

JODI HAYWOOD - Essay 46

TRACY AABEY-HAMMOND - Art 50

LEIGHA BASINI - Essay 52

ANNA CAVANAGH - Essay 56

JAMIE LYNN - Art 58

SOOJUNG JO - Poetry 60

MATTHEW SALESSES - Essay 62

MILA C. KONOMOS - Poetry 66

DIANE WHEATON - Essay 76

KIMBERLY MCKEE, PHD - Essay 80

BEATA SKONECKI, LMSW - Essay 86

NICOLE J. BURTON - Essay 88

CECILIA HEIMEE FLUMÉ - Art 90

ELIZABETH COLE - Essay 92

ROSITA GONZALÉZ - Art 94

WENDY M. LAYBOURN - Essay 98

CATHERINE A. JOHNSTON - Essay 102

STEPHEN DAVID LUKESON - Poetry 106

LARRY CLOW - Essay 108

LYNN GRUBB - Essay 112

LIZ SEMONS - Lyrics 116

CHRISTINE SATORY - Art 120

KAYE PEARSE - Essay 124

MI OK SONG BRUINING - Poetry 126

JOSHUA CROME - Essay 134

AMIRA ROSE DAVIS - Poetry 136

ZARA PHILLIPS - Essay & Lyrics 142

CHRISTOPHER WILSON - Essay 146

DARYN WATSON - Essay 148

ANNEGHEM WALL - Poetry 152

GRACE NEWTON - Essay 154

SARAH ELIZABETH GREER - Essay 156

MEI-MEI AKWAI ELLERMAN, PHD - Art 164

SHANNON GIBNEY - Essay 170

JULIE STROMBERG - Essay 172

SUSAN HARRIS O'CONNOR, MSW - Essay 174

M. C. MALTEMPO - Essay 178

Contributers 188

Editors 199

Dedication

I MAGINE THAT YOU ARE WALKING through the countryside. Suddenly you raise your eyes and behold an enormous tree, laden with lush, ripe red apples, all different shapes and sizes as it has flourished in the wild. Each lustrous apple began as a tiny bud that opened up into a perfect, delicate white blossom. Despite torrential rains, buffeting winds, periods of drought under the hot scorching sun, every flower has grown into a heavenly scented unique fruit.

Dear Reader, each one of you was born perfect, exquisite to behold, destined to develop into an amazing, resilient, gifted individual. Each one of you, though likely faced with painful, harrowing as well as exhilarating challenges, will not only survive, but will thrive.

This volume of deeply personal experiences, courageously shared by dozens of adopted and fostered adults, is our gift to you. As you follow our journeys, distinct yet linked by innumerable common threads, we hope that you will come upon at least one, if not several, accounts or feelings captured in the raw that speak to you because they mirror struggles and feats of your own.

Each writer and artist has discarded layers of expectations upheld by societal norms, directly or indirectly supported by adoptive family members or self-imposed. While in search of our true selves, our authentic being, we have wrestled with issues of identity, racism, lack of self esteem, rejection, loneliness, otherness, trauma, and the very definition of "being adopted" or "adoptees."

Through the immense power of the written word-private stories, poems, lyrics, and figurative arts-paintings, drawings, photographs and ceramics, each of us has fought fierce battles to discover and claim our identity and affirm our authentic selfhood. We have gone through a deep internal shift and debunked the stereotypical images of what it means and feels like to be adopted, according to the so-called experts. We have 'flipped the script!' not just in strictly personal terms, but as a vast, collective, creating a ripple effect that extends beyond national boundaries. We invite you to join us, via this anthology, in the rapidly expanding *Flip the Script* movement. You will have our heartfelt support as you face your inner demons, and venture forth to discover your true self, becoming a change-maker in the process.

May you find comfort and inspiration in your outspoken and indomitable counter parts which over the years blossomed. We are rediscovering our original beauty: the beauty of apple blossoms in spring that mature into life-giving and sustaining fruit whose seeds will propagate for generations to come.

-Mei-Mei Akwai Ellerman, PhD

November –
flip the script

power struggle

process w/someone
equal with

sharing narrative diff
creating narrative add

Foreword

WE HAVE COME FULL CIRCLE, and this is how it began …

Like many, I discovered that finding my original family was much harder than I imagined. In the summer of 2014, I visited Korea for the first time since my departure in 1968. Full of hope and aspirations, I discovered not only the comfort Korea offered in food— but the added emotional comfort of visiting with a group of adult adoptees. Every triumph of reunion was felt by us all. Every affirmation of loss closed our ranks.

I returned to the U.S. invigorated by my experiences in Korea but also broken by all the unknowns … my birth family, my actual birthdate, my birth story.

In my grief, I was quiet. Upon my return, my teenage son spiraled into an anxious frenzy. I had missed his first week of high school where he was suffering from bullying and the academic pressures from a highly competitive high school environment. My husband took off on a jet plane to Korea for business, and my son broke down.

I was now the mother alone with her feelings shelved.

In the first moments of my son's breakdown, as the emergency staff and others questioned my mothering abilities, I flashed back to my imagined childhood where my own first mother lost the ability to protect me and care for me.

I was becoming her.

In the next month, October, we consistently visited emergency rooms and clinics. My son called suicide hotlines; the police questioned my parenting numerous times. I felt hopeless, but my life as a mother had importance. My daughter was also suffering; if I could not help my son, I could envelop her. Her needs gave me strength. We are a family of means— that privilege served me as a mother on her own in the United States.

Additionally, the *Dear Wonderful You, Letters to Adopted & Fostered Youth* anthology project was gearing up. The adoptee community supported me and invigorated me; my activism grew. *Dear Wonderful You* had given adult adoptees a collective voice. During the taping of the promotional video for the book, my fellow editor, Amanda Woolston, made a statement that set in my mind. The earworm … '*It's time we flip that script.*'

As November approached, I sought help from a mental health professional. I expressed my feelings of inadequacy as a mother, a daughter and an adoptee. I explained how my loyalties to please the media, adoption agencies and adoptive parents had eaten away at my self-esteem.

My visit to Korea had solidified my longing to be comfortable in my own skin. While my search left many unanswered questions, one known fact haunted me. My birthday in November was a fabrication. Top that fact with the looming "celebration" of adoption during "National Adoption Awareness Month"... and the poignant missing voices of adult adoptees in *November*.

It was crushing.

With encouragement from my mental health clinician, I proposed a media campaign to my *Lost Daughters' sisters*; the *Lost Daughters* is an online collective of women writers who are all adult adoptees. The group discusses topics around domestic and international adoption. I asked my sisters to help me elevate the voices of adult adoptees for the entire month of November. Many of them had never been on Twitter when I asked them to take the 130 characters and express their complexities with the hashtag #FliptheScript on National Adoption Month.

At a time when I limped along, the voices of not only my sisters, but the brave ones, the ones who often were silent, took the Twitter floor, flooded Facebook and garnered the attention of mainstream media. Celebrities and journalists embraced their own narratives as adoptees and shared their stories.

As I read all of the brave narratives, in those 130 characters, a flood of comfort engulfed me and washed my recent wounds. Their words filled the cracks in my psyche. As a collective we became stronger. I shed the niceties I had used to hide my pain as their brevity helped me to become more vocal and truthful.

The adult adoptee writers of this project gave me strength to weather this past year. I lost my adoptive father. I discovered the secrets of my adoptive family ... that my late father had a son with a Korean woman a year before my birth. And my husband and I moved our little family to Korea for a five-month journey.

The trauma and the comfort mix in Korea for me today, just as they did for me in November of 2014. Much of the pain of the last year has been tempered by your voices ... adult adoptee voices.

Adoptees are strong. Hear them here, and they will strengthen you as well.

- Rosita González

JOE SOLL 조 살, LCSW
ART & ESSAY

REUNION:
Medium: Acrylic on Canvas

Finding Myself

What I knew about being an adoptee growing up was that I was unlovable.
What I know now is that I was and am lovable.

What I knew about being an adoptee growing up was that I could not talk about my feelings about being adopted.
What I know now is that I must talk about my feelings about being adopted.

What I knew about being an adoptee growing up was that I was unworthy.
What I know now is that I am as worthy as anyone else.

What I knew about being an adoptee growing up was that I was from another planet.
What I know now is that I am a member of the human race.

What I knew about being an adoptee growing up was I was not born, just 'materialized.'
What I know now is that I was born, I truly exist.

What I knew about being an adoptee growing up was I was illegitimate.
What I know now is that no baby is illegitimate.

What I knew about being an adoptee growing up was I heard people refer to me as a bastard so that was a part of my identity.
What I know now is that how I was conceived does not change who I am.

What I knew about being an adoptee growing up was that I was not allowed to express feelings about it.
What I know now about being an adoptee is that all my feelings are valid, that no feelings are ever wrong and that it is always ok to express them.

What I knew about being an adoptee growing up was that I was not allowed to talk about my first mother.
What I know now about being an adoptee is that it's normal to want to talk about my first mother.

What I knew about being an adoptee growing up was that I was supposed to make my adoptive parents happy.
What I know now about being an adoptee is that I am not responsible for their happiness.

What I knew about being an adoptee growing up was that I was supposed to be happy on my birthday but I was not.
What I know now about being an adoptee is that I can choose what I feel on my birthday. I can use it as a day of mourning and I can choose another day to celebrate being alive.

What I knew about being an adoptee growing up was that I was chosen, perhaps from a baby supermarket.
What I know now about being an adoptee growing up was that my parents chose to adopt me and each time they told me I was chosen, it caused me pain, reminding me that I lost my mother when I was born,

What I knew about being an adoptee growing up was that I was special, but it made me sad to hear it.
What I know now about being an adoptee is that every time I heard the word 'special', it caused me pain, reminding me that I lost my mother when I was born,

What I knew about being an adoptee growing up was that I was lucky, but it made me sad to hear it.
What I know now about being an adoptee is that every time I heard the word 'lucky', it caused me pain, reminding me that I lost my mother when I was born.

What I knew about being an adoptee growing up was that I was always in pain and angry at my adoptive parents for not understanding why I hurt.
What I know now as an adoptee is that my adoptive parents had no way of knowing that I was in pain from losing my natural mother.

What I knew about being an adoptee growing up was that my natural mother died in a car-crash.
What I know now as an adoptee is that my adoptive parents were told by a therapist to make up the car-crash story.

What I knew about being an adoptee growing up was that I would hurt forever.
What I know now as an adoptee is that I can heal.

What I knew about being an adoptee growing up was deep shame that I was adopted.
What I know now as an adoptee is that there is no shame in being adopted.

What I knew about being an adoptee growing up was that my mother didn't want me.
What I know now as an adoptee that searched is that my mother didn't want to lose me.

What I knew about being an adoptee growing up was that I was not allowed to be who I was.
What I know now as an adoptee, and perhaps most important of all, is that it is ok to be me.

KEVIN MINH ALLEN

ESSAY

I Am Nothing
(AND THAT IS SOMETHING)

A T ONE POINT WHILE DRIVING on Route 395, nearing Susanville, California, on my way to Reno, Nevada, I veered onto the wide highway shoulder and came to a stop. Dusk was settling in, darkness was prevailing, and no other cars were on the winding road except for mine. The moon was a thin crescent sitting in a black void. The pitch dark land stretched for miles on end in every direction and nothing seemed to be stirring out in that featureless expanse. I was so tempted to get my backpack out of the trunk and just walk toward the steel-cold purplish-orange horizon until I couldn't see the car anymore behind me. Such soothing emptiness and silence beckoned to me like the promise of a Paradise where I wouldn't mind disappearing forever. This was in December 2013, and I was reaching my 40th year of life on this planet. I was seeking solace and relief from ever-changing circumstances, and I was seeking a way to a better understanding of how far I've come.

I was born either face-up or face-down, either screaming until I was red in the face or holding in all my breath until my body turned blue. Either my mother was given the chance to hold me within the first few minutes of my birth and look upon my face or I was given over to someone else's outstretched arms and placed in a room crammed with other bawling newborns to stare at a ceiling fan blurring the air as it rotated. Either my father was there in the room to count my toes and fingers or he was a ghost just like my mother. I couldn't tell you because I just don't know. Or perhaps I would know the whole story if someone who witnessed my entrance into the world could get word to me. But, I've been told before that that is asking for far too much.

There are no quick and easy answers as to why I chose to celebrate such a momentous stage in my life by myself. All I knew is that I just wanted to drive very far away from where I lived and worked, far away from the familiar. I had decided that I wanted no friends and no family around me to celebrate the supposed day of my birth; I really didn't want anyone at all to revel with me and celebrate my sometimes quick and sometimes slow accumulation of years in this space I temporarily occupy. In order to properly commemorate this significant year of birth, I thought, I needed to be alone, on my own.

I live with no illusions. Most likely, my parents are dead. That is the Unknown I believe in because I fear that the Truth will never ring true to me. Mind you, I don't mean that they are dead to me. In the moving pictures of my mind I imagine them talking. Without any sort of mementos or photographs of them to go on, I pretend their conversations revolve around reliving the moment when they wished they had, or had not, met in Vietnam, kissed in Vietnam, made love in Vietnam, and met their demise in Vietnam. My memories of my parents are fantasies, little tall tales I tell myself every time my reflection sees itself on the other side of the mirror. I have no trouble recognizing myself, but I probably would never recognize either one of my parents, even if they passed by me on the same side of the street. *When they left me, I left them.* I disappeared into another land, another language, another family. Thigh-high snow drifts in the winter and raucous pool parties in the summer are what I grew up with— not wilting palm trees and morning alms to shuffling monks outside the temple.

In an essay I wrote almost a decade ago, I ended it by writing, "I slipped into this world, and I will slip out of it." It's a clever thought, albeit a nihilistic one. I still feel this way whenever life lets me down, but I eventually balance things out by realizing that there doesn't have to be a grand, overriding reason for me to live my life as I see fit. There may not be any real reason for me existing in this particular place and at this exact time. The road trip was a momentous way to bring me out of myself and then back around to myself to understand that I'm doing alright in the world. My father and my mother may be gone, but I'm still here, their son.

I am nothing. I am nothing but a man who drives 14 hours to a city in the dead of winter where no one knows him and no one ever will.

SUSAN ITO

ESSAY

Enough

TODAY IS MOTHER'S DAY. A day of all ambivalence— of love, pain, longing, and regret. A day of ordinary moments. Two mothers.

I wake up and carry a vase full of flowers down to the kitchen. My 92 year old adoptive mother is already up and ready for church. She's already made her Lipton tea and toast. I couldn't get up early enough to make her breakfast in bed. I've never been able to, even as a child. She has beaten me to the kitchen table every morning of my life. She exclaims at the flowers, red and pink roses, studded with fluffy chrysanthemums. Her name in Japanese means "chrysanthemum." She thanks me with enthusiasm. I want to say something about how much I appreciate her mothering me, all the ways she's cared for me, but the words are stuck. We don't talk about things like this. Our relationship skates on the surface, like slippery black ice. I give her what she enjoys – flowers, and later, chocolate. I want her to be happy.

I fear she will never really be happy.

My adoptive mother is 92 years old. My birthmother, whom I searched for and met over 30 years ago, is 82. I am acutely aware that each interaction that I have, with each of them, could be the last. Will there come a morning when my adoptive mother will not be able to climb the fourteen carpeted steps from her bedroom? Would my birthmother's family – my half siblings, her husband – notify me if anything happened to her? Last year, she fell and shattered her femur. She emailed me after she was discharged from the hospital, after the surgery that pinned her bones, but nobody else had let me know.

Decades ago, when I was in college and barely twenty years old, both of my mothers and I shared a Mother's Day lunch in a sushi restaurant in Manhattan. It was strange and surreal, dreamlike and excruciating. I think I acted like a brat. I think I engaged in a terrible mental game of compare-and-contrast in which nobody could possibly win. It filled me up and it broke my heart. It was the only day we ever spent in each other's presence. We all wore a trench coat, which amuses me when I look at the photograph my father snapped. Mine was dark green, and my mothers' were both beige. I stood to the side of them; my mouth was twisted in an awkward smile.

This year, I sent my birthmother a delivery of tulips. Tulips... because she grew up in a small town that celebrated those flowers with an annual festival.

When I first met her, she said— we'll have to go there together at tulip time. I must show you. But it's been over thirty years and that trip never happened. It was a little subversive of me, ordering flowers to be delivered on Saturday, the day *before* Mother's Day. I'm sure she doesn't know that it's also known as Birth Mothers' Day. It was declared by a group of birth mothers who wanted it to be acknowledged that in order for many adoptive mothers to *have* a Mother's Day to celebrate at all, it was necessary for other mothers to first conceive, birth and let go of those children.

I enclosed a card that said simply, "Thinking of you. Happy Mother's Day." She emailed back, "Thank you. They're beautiful."

That's all we can do. But this year... she attached a photo of herself. I haven't seen her in almost ten years. She's aged, but she still looks regal and elegant. I noticed that her signature bangs, which she'd worn since childhood, have grown out. She still wears fashionable, slightly Asianesque outfits. Her gleaming dark wood dining room table is clean and clutter-free.

When I first visited her house, it felt like a beautifully curated museum. Careful and elegant. The house in which was raised was one step away from an episode of Hoarders. We also had beautiful Asian artifacts, but they were behind cartons of my salesman father's samples – cloisonné jewelry, stuffed animals, baskets, banners, and little souvenir state spoons. Later, avalanching mountains of junk mail, flyers, bills, magazines and newspapers covered everything. It was a fortress of paper. We also owned a gleaming dark dining room table, but I only saw its surface twice in my life. It was covered by flannel covered "table protectors," and then a plastic tablecloth. I gasped when I finally saw the cherry wood underneath, decades later.

My birth mother continues to keep my existence cocooned in secrecy. This hurts, but it has subsided into a chronic, persistent ache. She flies thousands of miles to a city less than a dozen miles from my home. Her visits are a flurry of social engagements, dinners and parties. I'm not invited. I wonder if she can feel my presence, pulsing across the water. I wonder if she feels regret. Once she said that regretted ever agreeing to meet me. I know that I am a can of worms.

I haven't stopped poking that question with every sharp stick I could find: Who is my birth father? *Who who who who who?* And while she never relented to my various forms of torture, she never gave up his name; I may have found it myself. But I realize, in my fifty-fifth year, that I am tired. I am tired of longing and reaching out for connection where there is none to be had.

My adoptive mother, for reasons I will never understand, has distanced herself, and by extension me, from every living relative we have. We live on our tiny island with my husband and daughters. She, like my birthmother, has a lifelong, spectacular patience and ability to hold her breath, to hold a grudge. She didn't speak to her youngest brother, my uncle, for decades. They were still estranged when he died.

I feel involuntarily estranged from so many members of my family. Because I am a searching adoptee, I am also a professional online stalker. I gaze at the children of my half-siblings, nephews and nieces by blood, through what passageways I can find. Their faces startle me, especially when I see echoes of my own children in their expressions, their eyes. I have never been an aunt to any of them. I long to reach out. But I won't cross my birth mother's familial picket line.

By some miracle, I married into a family that embraces me without hesitation, condition or judgment. The fact that they acknowledge me as kin is stunning to me. They have written my name in permanent pen onto their family tree. They call out to me on social media and my eyes smart with grateful tears. "Hey cousin!"

When I was a child, my life was entangled with my cousins'. We spent every weekend together. I had my birthday parties there, on the concrete patio, with a clothesline hanging with powdered donuts, with paper donkeys and blindfolds. My cousins and I walked along the railroad tracks and picked armloads of pussy willows. It was later in my adolescence, when the trouble set in. Trouble between my mother and the sisters-in-law. Our shared vacations (Cape Cod with its frigid water and lobster rolls), family outings (apple picking with sushi picnics) and shared holidays dwindled down into holiday cards signed with no note. Even those evaporated and left silence.

I've wanted much from my mothers, from my families. To be acknowledged and seen. I've wanted information, the simplest of stories. Who was my father? How did I come to be? I've wanted affection and a mother's hand on my hair. I've wanted everything from them that I've tried to give my own daughters: a listening ear, an open heart, unwavering support.

In order to avoid crippling bitterness over all they haven't done or said or given or provided, I see the small and large things they have. My adoptive mother is not a talker or a sharer. But she is steadfast. She would die for me, and I know that. She leans on me. She makes me laugh almost every day, with her tough Brooklyn fists-up attitude that once made me cower. She is the core and the heart of our multigenerational family. We revolve around her, especially my children and husband love her in a less complicated way. She has taught my daughters endless patience and tenderness. She has given me a million chances to renew my love for her.

My birth mother has approached and receded like the tide, sometimes in cycles that span years. She has fought to remain hidden, out of fear and shame. I understand that. I would love to have all of my medical records, and a birth story, and connection with my biological nieces and nephews. To know my father's name and a chance to know his family. But I see the shame. I see how it has taken all she has to maintain the thinnest thread of connection to me. I see how that is brave. I know that for her to send me an email with her photograph attached was huge. She let herself be seen, just a little bit more.

We're all getting older. My own children are adults now, in their twenties. One of them brought me a Mother's Day bowl of fruit salad, with the bananas omitted, because she knows they disgust me. The other made me a plate of bacon and poached eggs. She lay in bed next to me, like she did as a toddler, and let me smell her coconut scented hair as I lay in bed, writing.

In the evening, we go out for Mother's Day dinner. The waterfront restaurant is crowded. It seems that everyone and their mother are there. Even though we have a reservation, we have to wait twenty minutes for our table. Her shoes keep falling off as she dangles her feet from the chair. She's so short her feet don't touch the ground. My mother is confused about what to order and then forgets what she tells the waitress. She is surprised when they bring her a prime rib that fills the plate; the ordeal of cutting the meat seems to bewilder her. Her granddaughters help. The restaurant, right on the estuary, is beautiful, and she seems glad to sit there at sundown with us: me, my husband, our daughters, and the boyfriend of one of them. We are all here. We order a key lime pie for dessert, generous with whipped cream and we use five forks to share it and she is happy. She tells us about the first time she ever tasted key lime pie, in Florida. We know the story. We have heard it often.

After dinner, we give her cards and her favorite treats, chocolate covered marshmallows. She reads the one line I've written in my card. "Thank you for being my mother." She keeps re-reading it, opening and closing the card. Every time she puts it down she looks at me and says, in a surprised voice, "Thank *you*. That's nice." It's a tiny little thread of communication, acknowledging something. I take it. My daughter gives me a hand-carved stamp of owls, and some exquisite cards, and a pair of Van Gogh patterned socks.

This year, it is a soft Mother's Day. It's a day of finally understanding that as flawed as they both are, my mothers are human, nearing the ends of their lives in which they have tried their best. They have, neither of them, acted in ways that I'd wished for. But I'm not going to be grudgey. I don't want to punish them. I want to quietly be with them, in whatever limited ways they can offer, and know that it is enough.

ADEL KSK

ART

TWO OF A KIND

Medium: Indian ink on arches paper

FOETUS LAND FOR SINKING WOMAN (Private Collection)
Medium: Indian ink on arches paper

WINTER SEEDLING (Private Collection)
Medium: Indian ink on arches paper

APRIL DINWOODIE

ESSAY

My Adoption Experience — What I Have Learned

M Y LIFE BEGAN WHEN I was born, not when I was adopted.

For many years and sadly, sometimes even today, adoptions are transacted in a way that does not allow for an understanding of or connectivity to families of origin. My 'birth' certificate lists my adoptive parents not my biological parents and even as a kid I found that odd. It did not in any way mean I did not love my parents or consider them my parents but...What happened between 1971 (my birth year) and 1973 (the year the certificate is dated)? Who were the two people who were fundamentally responsible for me being on the planet? Who were the people who took care of me for several months during my temporary foster care placement and with whom I spent my first Christmas? These people matter because they are a part of me; and all parts of a life matter. It took a long time to unravel both practically and emotionally that there was fundamental loss in gaining my adoptive family that love and cherish me and that I love and cherish right back. I am currently piecing together my beginnings and will have to do so without my biological mother's perspective - she left the planet before I had a chance to meet her. My hope is that both professionals and parents embrace openness more and more allowing adopted people the access to the information and connectivity that fundamentally belongs to them and is part of them. We can't love all parts if we do not know all parts.

Adoption is one word defined by many distinct realities.

For many years my adoption experience was all I knew. For a brief time, as a kid, I thought every family had at least one adopted kid and usually, that kid was brown. When no other brown adopted kids showed up at school, I realized that my family may indeed be unique. As my life unfolded and I gained connections to a community of people with the shared experience of adoption, I learned that the definition of adoption is simple but the realities of the lived experience are anything but. From foster care adoption to private domestic adoption to inter-country adoption - I have learned that how, where and why you enter into the adoption experience (and whether you have control over certain factors or not) matters and that even with a common bond our distinct realities differ as first/birth parents, adoptive parents and adopted people. One simple word that connects us, many unique lived experiences define us.

Being part of a larger community matters.

Adoption is a uniquely personal experience. I have learned the simple truths that if you have not experienced adoption personally, try as you might, it is likely you won't fully understand it. As an adopted person, my life has been transformed by having other members of the adoption community as some of my dearest friends, partners, colleagues and confidants. I was not exposed to the wider world of adopted people, first/birth parents, adoptive parents and professionals until I was in my mid-twenties and starting my search in earnest. I have learned that my comrades in adoption can be my lifeline when no one else understands. There is a sense of calm in knowing that I do not even have to explain, they get it. Connecting children to these communities as early as possible can be transformational. I have learned firsthand how life-changing sharing in the common bond of adoption can be at any age but it is most beautiful when I see it unfold with young people. Although all of our stories are distinct, there is a common bond in living adoption.

Perceptions, policies and practices must be reformed.

The general public's perceptions of adoption are often shaped by polarizing news stories or Hollywood depictions of the fairytale or the nightmare. While there is no doubt some adoption narratives make great headlines, so many people experiencing adoption do not live the headlines in their everyday lives. Most of us live somewhere in between and all of us would benefit from more understanding and more modern sensibilities surrounding the realities of adoption. In the absence of uniform best practices and vastly different policies state by state, professionals, parents and adopted people are often left to navigate the complexity of their realities without the support they need. Even after decades of lived experience and research from Donaldson Adoption Institute (DAI) and others, adoption is so often treated like a one-time transaction instead of a lifelong transformation. We know what to do; now we need to actually start doing it.

The adoption community is more powerful together.

I have learned there is power in numbers. Changing perspectives and truly employing what we know from research and lived experience to ensure families are stronger will take a concerted effort. Unraveling the powerful and longstanding entities that are counting on the fact that as a community we will remain fractured and less strong means we need to find every opportunity to stand together. Our different experiences make us a rich tapestry and finding the connecting points where we can agree and come together will be critical as we move forward. Together we can accelerate positive change in how people perceive, think and behave about adoption— making it about people instead of process. Together, we can make adoption about building strong families instead of just building toward a final court date. Together, we can show the world that adoption is not a mere transaction, but a lifelong transformation.

LUCY CHAU LAI-TUEN
POETRY & MIXED MEDIA

I Know This Face

I know this uncharted face
A topography worthy of exploration
An epidermal physiognomy that has lost so much
and not just in translation
A miss-placed blueprint
As I scan the image
Wondering which features I share with the Mother I never knew
How similar is my face to my Mother's?
A face that my fingers-tips will never caress
Nor trace the curve of her cheek
Or feel the flush of her skin
The provenance of my face is unknown
My eyes will never linger over the image of my creator
This face will never see myself in my mother's eyes
Or turn over a sepia crackled photograph
Puzzling over the copper-plate script that says
So-and-so on this date with Mum
Do I age as my Mother did?
Time drags both skin and memories towards the earth
what passing relevance is left?
What would the Mother of my face recognise?
The eyebrow?
The forehead?
The mouth?
And seeing my face then say,
"That's my daughter."
I have long surrendered any hope of seeing
Myself in my Mother's eyes
Of taking tea in an unfamiliar front room
Feeling the clear water-weak coloured sunshine of a winter afternoon

Or pausing with nerves alert to every minor sensation as I ask
"Are you really my Mother?"
Scenarios play in my head
Dreams of reunion
I run in slow motion through softly defused colours towards my Mother
Waking instead to the mute motherless tones of reality
I have travelled unaware with the pain of accumulated years
Does my Mother still walk with measured steps across some path?
The meaning of the word Mother is lost
Almost impossible for me to grasp
In all the intervening years I have not felt any anger towards my Mother
Sadness and emptiness of spirit haunt me
As the unknown ghost of my Mother's lost smile
The silent breathing of an unoccupied chair
Has my Mother passed?
Looking at this image
Eying with age and experience
All my losses and regrets neatly unpacked
I see every individual image
Interlocking, intersecting, merging, connecting, aligning
Forming one complete picture
I cannot change the past
But I can affect my future
I can write my own script
Flipping the picture
And on the back write
To my darling daughter with much love
Mum

How To Get To The Han River

FROM THE GRANDLY NAMED LUXURY Apartments off Choen'ho Subway Station, take a right next to Holly's Coffee Shop, where you can order a Latte and the counter girls will giggle at your guidebook-learned Korean, your horrid *hanguk mal*, and smile shyly. Not long ago it was rare to see a coffee shop in Seoul, but now on every corner you will notice not only a Caribou Coffee, but also a Dunkin Donuts, a Kentucky Fried Chicken, a Pizza Hut, and now this Starbucks-wannabe coffee shop in what was once a land of tea drinkers. You will also notice more overweight children than you would have 20 years ago, more signs in English, more dairy products on billboards and television, and though some would insist that there's no connection between these things, others believe that there is. And, even though you are an adoptee and carry the requisite anxiety upon returning, venture forth, tell yourself it seems silly to be afraid of your homeland, your lost language, your own people; and from there walk for blocks down a crowded Seoul alley, which isn't so much an alley but a bustling street; and down this alley you will be passed on either side by *ajummahs* and *ajashi* hauling home plastic bags, by pale-skinned girls holding carefully manicured hands with other pale-skinned girls; by scooters and trucks that shouldn't be able to fit down this alley yet somehow do, by dogs almost too small to be respectable in America. Take note of every landmark you can, any bit of English you can— Mini-stop, Mao's Restaurant, Cake Parlor, Kia Motors, Olive Young— so that hopefully you can find your way back, until you reach the Han River.

You may have read in your guidebooks that Koreans are group-oriented, that they think a person sitting alone is odd— especially a woman. Only *ajummahs* and *ajashi* sit alone in parks, afforded that privilege by age, wisdom, and time. As if to underline the point, groups of elders gather under bridges by the Han River for as far as you can see. Boisterous packs of *ajashi* sing songs and talk loudly, while *ajummahs* nearby laugh at them and with them in the slightly dismissive way that older women do when they are beyond flirting, beyond prettiness, beyond caring what others think. You might be surprised by how much you envy them, how they seem settled in their bodies, the way they mirror each other's faces, how they belong here in ways that you do not, but mostly that they have what you do not have, that they grew up here and live here and will probably die here. You may have thought you'd gotten beyond all that, that the talk about adoption grief was just romanticized exaggeration of the orphan myth as told by media, literature, and pop culture, but within those overwrought *Joy Luck Club*-style tears, lives an essence of truth, that to lose one's history and homeland is undeniably tragic.

So eat and shop. They say that many adoptees have "food issues," sensitivities to certain things beyond lactose intolerance and the ubiquitous alcohol red-face, preoccupations, eating disorders, tendencies towards hoarding, and that these are remnants of our fragile beginnings, of starting life in orphanages, in foster care, malnourished, sickly. There are stories of adoptees hiding food under beds and in drawers, eating too much or too little, or not at all. Perhaps you were always in the former camp, never met a food you didn't like. Koreans also love to eat, your guidebooks say, because for so long they were a poor country without much food, and like so many things about Korea, you have to trust what someone else tells you, you who are a tourist in your homeland. So, in this love for food you might feel slightly more Korean, in the same way that riding the subway alone might make you feel Korean, blending into the crowd, talking to no one, just another face on Line 2, and consuming makes you feel thus comforted.

Another aspect to consuming might surprise you, however, how it feels familiar, so American, like putting on an old shirt or slipping into a warm towel, how just standing in the underground Co-Ex Mall puts a recognizable stamp on your Seoul experience; *they have the same shit there that we have at here*, John Travolta told Samuel L. Jackson in <u>Pulp Fiction</u>, *but it's just a little different*. And then there's Konglish, that particularly Korean use of English letters, like the Aquarium snack bar that's named Very Very Sea, or the t-shirts proclaiming, "Life Your Happiness" and "Grudge Grudge Grudge," *the same shit just a little different*. So take your time, wander the streets back from the Han River to the apartment building, buzzing from the bright yellow lights and ocean of faces, the high-pitched pop music and the children running everywhere, and keep eating and consuming. The act of purchasing will make you feel safe. There's also a slight feeling of superiority in the transaction, undeniable, immutable, slightly shameful, in which a service is being performed for you, alleviating some of your feelings of inferiority.

"Just think of yourself like a deaf mute," an adoptee friend advises, "and you'll have an easier time getting around. Don't try to use your limited Korean. It just confuses them when they try to speak to you."

Follow her advice, and for the most part it will work well. Indeed, the younger generation seems rather amused and conciliatory towards you, their linguistically ignorant *kyopo* cousin, offering up their school-learned English with helpful enthusiasm— "Do you want a basket?" the boy at the Mini-mart asks, indicating the plastic bags, "Will you take it away?" the girl at Holly's Coffee inquires— even the older workers, although less friendly, at least will not yell at you, which is the real fear, the possibility of someone publicly shaming you for not speaking Korean, because every adoptee has experienced an older Korean person scolding her for not speaking her native tongue. The difficulty in such exchanges lies in ascertaining whether the behavior is cultural, personal, or just particular to that person— you would only be able to guess, for example, what may have gone wrong if an old woman swatted at a your behind as you walked up the subway stairs— were you walking too slow or too fast, too much on the right or the left? Is there a Korean way to exit the subway? Or was she just a grumpy old woman? Such is the paradox of being an adoptee in Korea. Your face says that you should understand how to exist in this country, how to order food, buy clothes, walk, and talk, but your life experience, your language, and your culture determine that you do not.

If it begins to rain, allow this, like shopping, to comfort you, how the water clears the air, how hiding under an umbrella creates solitude, space, and anonymity. Allow yourself to feel a fleeting solidarity with those around you as you hurry home, seeking shelter; but like every time that you may have felt more Korean on this trip, it is artificial, this connection with your homeland imagined to help you cope with your alienation from it.

But, if there should come a day when you get the chance to trek up Pongwha Mountain to make offerings to your ancestors, take it, and bring along some adoptee friends. You may have been told that Buddhist shrines sit on top where locals pray, so buy *soju* and fruit, learn the proper way to worship. And, if by mistake you end up in a nearby exercise park, because none of you knows exactly where the mountain is, and all around you are groves of trees, the ends of which are wrapped in white paper, and not one of you knows what kind of trees they are, and something inside you feels guilty for not knowing, like the knowing is somehow Korean, unlike you, then you should find a secluded bench. And, if by chance someone has left a scarf with roses painted on it, you should take it as a sign, a gift, and make the scarf and the bench your altar and make the offerings, anyway. You should sit there afterward in silence, the connection real this time. Even if it isn't with '*Korean* Koreans', as you sometimes call them, it's at least with someone who looks like you. Allow the mosquitoes to nibble at your legs, mosquitoes that seem bigger, faster, and smarter than their American cousins. Sit there until your legs are covered in bites, as the mosquitoes happily take your blood and you give it to them freely.

LAURA COTTER

ESSAY

Fireworks Across The Sky

I USED TO SEE MYSELF AS a fortune cookie. Early in my junior year of high school, when I was asked to create a "non-representational" self-portrait in art class, I drew a fortune cookie for two reasons. First, people think that fortune cookies are Asian, but they are really American. They were invented in California in the early 1900s. And second, the fortune inside the cookie represents fate and luck, both of which played a defining role at the beginning of my life. I was adopted at thirteen months old from an orphanage in China, but American culture is really all I have ever known.

During that same year, I was trying to develop a meaningful project to cap my twelve years in Girl Scouts. I knew that my older sister, who is very connected to her Chinese identify, was leading a trip to China that summer for Chinese adoptees. They were going to volunteer at the Half the Sky China Care Home, a facility that provides medical and other care to orphans with special needs. I conceived a plan to involve various local communities to learn to knit, and then to knit winter hats for the children at the China Care home. I figured that my sister could deliver the hats.

The project was very successful and many beautiful hats were created. But along the way, both my mom and my sister asked me if I might want to deliver the hats myself. The idea began to grow on me. Four months later I, along with eleven other Chinese adoptees and a suitcase full of knitted hats, was travelling to Beijing to volunteer at the China Care Home.

We were just about to take a tour of the home when a five-year old boy came running up yelling "Jiejie! Jiejie! Baowo!" ("Sister! Sister! Pick me up!"). He stood surveying us and pointing to which "jiejies" he wanted. He told us his name was ChangMing, and he tried to convince us that he was eight years old. He was at China Care because he has fused fingers and toes. I instantly fell in love with this energetic little boy.

The children in my assigned room, other than ChangMing, ranged in age from nine months to two years. There were children being treated for clubfoot, cleft lip and palate, heart defects, autism, and spina bifida. It was shocking at first to see some of the children with more severe physical issues, but when they smiled and laughed, nothing else mattered but making them smile again. They were easy to love and so quick to return the love.

One child, who we nicknamed "Scooter," had a cute little smile and chubby cheeks and reminded me of pictures of me when I was little. Another boy who was called "Er Pang" (Second Fat) reminded me of a nickname that I had at my orphanage. One of the few stories I know from my early life in China is that the nannies nicknamed me "Pang DiZhu" (Fat Landlord) because I was not shy about demanding food and attention.

With each child that I met, my own beginnings in China came into sharper focus. I did not face the challenges that many of these children face, but I felt a deep connection to our shared beginnings as Chinese orphans. I went on this trip thinking that I was going to be helping the children, but it turns out that they were helping me to realize that being Chinese is an integral and undeniable part of who I am.

I spent much of my time with ChangMing, the boy that I met that first day. Every morning I would walk down the hallway to his room, and he would be waiting by the gate. The moment he saw me he would start jumping up and down screaming "Jiejie! Jiejie!" and run down the hall to meet me. He led me around the China Care Home and always stopped to look back to see if I was following him. One day ChangMing came in wearing a small version of the volunteer shirts that we were required to wear. He ran over to me saying, "Jiejie, womenyiyang" ("sister, we're the same").

If I were asked to do that art project self-portrait again, I would not draw a fortune cookie. I would draw fireworks. Fireworks were invented in China and mark the celebrations of the Chinese New Year and Chinese Labor Day (my birthday). But America has made fireworks distinctly its own. Fireworks are about celebration, coming together with family and friends, and commemorating our history. Like me, fireworks are one hundred percent Chinese *and* one hundred percent American. My new self-portrait would be colorful fireworks, marking their own path across the sky.

Epilogue

WHEN I RETURNED HOME AFTER volunteering with the Half the Sky China Care Home, I could not stop thinking about ChangMing. It was painful to think that I might never know how he was and what his future held. In December 2013, I learned through Half the Sky that he had returned to his home orphanage in Shenzhen but despite my efforts, I could not find any further information. Throughout the next year, I kept wondering about him, how he was, and whether he had been adopted. I started college in 2014 and I hung up a picture of him in my college dorm room. But over a year passed and, despite continual on-line searches by both my mom and me, there was no news of ChangMing.

In February 2015, something amazing happened. My mom found a blog by a family in Chicago detailing their adoption of ChangMing. Seeing that blog describing ChangMing's new family with his glowing smiles on every page, felt like a miracle. We reached out to them with a letter, enclosing pictures, and explaining how I had met ChangMing at the China Care Home. They wrote a very welcoming letter back and reported how excited ChangMing, now called Luke, was to hear from me. At the end of May, my mom, my sister and I traveled to Chicago to see Luke and meet his wonderful new family. He has five brothers and sisters, two of them also from China. We met them in Chicago and then visited their home for an evening, sharing a meal, playing baseball, and looking at photos. It was a surreal and wonderful experience, to be reunited with the little boy that I had met 2 years ago, halfway around the world, who played an important role in helping me embrace my own identity. It was an incredible and heartwarming experience to see that he has found a beautiful family.

MELISSA DAE SOOK KIM

ART

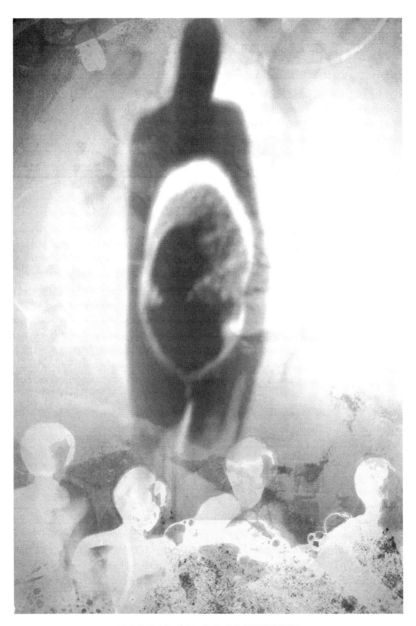

IN SEARCH OF IDENTITY

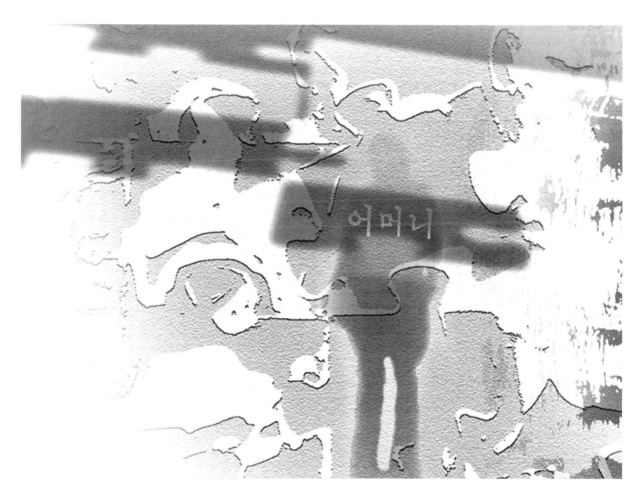

MISSING PIECE

Who Cut My Umbilical Cord?

Who cut my umbilical cord,
and tied it off into what is now
my deep belly button,
deep enough to hold grapes?

What happens to a baby when a mother gives birth all alone?
...It must happen.
It could happen, say, if
girl runs away
because she is not supposed to be pregnant.

She might run away
and live alone in the cliffs
overlooking the sea
when her belly starts showing.
She might go into the caves and give birth all alone.

She might love the child
for a few days until she realizes that her baby is starving,
...so she decides to

Leave the child on the street,
wrapped in a blanket to be found and fed
before returning to her family.

What happens if an umbilical cord is not cut?

Mama cats have teeth.
Do they do the separating with their teeth?
(for some reason, I do not think it is human nature to bite an amniotic sac

with our teeth and eat it like mama cats do...)
What if some mountain lion appeared,
demanding that he eat me – but my mother defended us both in the cave!?

What if, somehow,
during the close fight,
the mountain lion nipped so close,
that *he* is the one who clipped my umbilical cord?

JODI HAYWOOD

ESSAY

If I Could Write A Letter To My Younger Self

M Y YOUNGER SELF HAD THE misfortune of being adopted by a clueless middle-aged couple who would never have been approved to adopt if one, her aunt, hadn't been a blood relative of hers to begin with. They had no children and no experience with children. They didn't know what they were getting into. Imagine someone has never had a driving lesson or held a license, and but is given a temperamental used car. Except, the car is a human being who will spend her entire childhood and adolescence feeling disconnected from everybody around her.

If I could write to my younger self, I would tell her the whole story, not withholding even the most painful details.

I would erase from her mind every doubt that her real parents loved her—every fear that she wasn't good enough for her real mother to keep. I would remind her how much she was loved by the father she met at age twelve. I would find out where her adopting aunt kept the letters from both of her parents protesting the adoption, including one from her real mother asking for visiting rights. Her real mother would never have permitted the awful haircut her aunt made her get when she was eleven that chopped off the reddish-brown locks that once fell halfway down her back and cut them so short that she got mistaken for a boy.

My younger self never got to be anybody's little princess. Nobody told her she was pretty. Her aunt took her to dermatologists who prescribed pills and creams and lotions to clear up her complexion. None of these remedies proved completely effective, because at the root of her skin flare-ups lay the stress of trying to belong in a world where she didn't fit and pretending to be something she wasn't, and the strain of overriding the awareness that something deep down inside of her was not normal. She grew those bangs out until they reached the tip of her nose so nobody would know she wasn't looking them in the eye. She didn't want anyone to see the mirrors to her soul and expose the fact that she was just a phony pretending to be a normal human being.

I would speak to her unspoken fear that she has an undiagnosed learning disability—a barrier that makes life a constant uphill climb for her when everyone else seems to just coast along with nothing more troublesome than minor speed bumps in their path.

I would give her the word the doctors were fumbling for, *Autism*, when she was between five and seven years old. Their assessments described her high intelligence, her verbal aptitude, and her ease of speaking with adults using limited eye contact coupled with difficulty making friends in her own age group. Her talents for writing and drawing, the dichotomy of her distractibility and ability to hyper-focus on her interests, her tendency to "shut down," and her "lack of bonding" with her adopters, frustrated her aunt enough to bring her to the children's diagnostic center on her sixth birthday.

Her team of psychologists, neurologists and psychiatrists needed to know the similarities between her behavior and the criteria for Asperger's syndrome. They were on the right track when they suggested that her early family upheaval contributed to her "lack of bonding" to her adopters who did not disclose the truth of her origins until she was twelve and gave her very little time to adjust to this truth before she reunited with her father in the land of her birth.

I would assure her she was entitled to her whole story and that the memories she had but couldn't trust because her adopters' deceit, were real. My younger self needed extra time to process new information and being fed tiny pieces of her narrative took so much longer to assimilate it into her reality. She believed, due to her limited vision, "difficult" behavior and her aunt's treatment of her as a "problem," that her real parents gave her away because she was too much to handle. So they gave up and washed their hands of her. She would find out at reunion that this simply wasn't true.

I would help her decipher who really loves her for herself and who would rather change her into a more docile, manageable creature; who would use the autism diagnosis to help her succeed and who not to entrust with it. I would let her know there are resources in place that would make school easier for her and to allow her to learn in her own way instead of attempting to force her into "typical" methods.

I would give her the freedom to call her adopter "Aunt" instead of "Mom" and to walk in her own truth instead of being dragged forcibly along the paths her aunt chose. I would tell here where her aunt kept those all-important psychiatric records and the aforementioned letters from her real parents. I would make these documents available to her when she needed them—when they would have helped and reassured her—instead of her finding them after her aunt's death when she was in her mid-thirties. I would tell her to embrace the love and acceptance showed to her by her "Spiritual Mom" whom she met at the age of 13, starved for a mother's unconditional love, yet believing herself undeserving of that love and fearing she would be given away again. I would tell her to ignore her aunt's efforts to undermine that relationship, on the grounds that her aunt was jealous she'd bonded with a replacement mother figure and not with the one who took her from her homeland.

My younger self was not crazy, despite what she believed and what other people tried to make her believe about herself. People with autism are not "retarded," "crazy" or unaware of what's going on around them. My younger self knew she didn't fit into the space that everybody tried to wedge her into. She resisted her aunt's efforts to cut her down to size to reshape her to fit into that space. At the same time my younger self did not know who she was. She was denied the opportunity to know her past, her truth, and arrive at her own understanding of it.

I would gift to my younger self a stronger sense of identity than her aunt was willing to nurture—and they both suffered for it. Had her aunt been able to release her own ideal of who this niece she adopted should turn out to be, they could have reached some amicability. Instead, my younger self was forced down the path her aunt wanted—ballet lessons, crowded birthday parties, approved clothes, and strict rules. She wanted my younger self to become a librarian or computer programmer and not the forensic psychologist my younger self dreamed of becoming.

Those birthday parties and social situations were a source of stress and anxiety. My younger self was forced to play hostess to girls she had nothing in common with. Girls who she felt lived on a different planet. She was some visiting alien whose real parents had dropped her off in a strange land and either forgotten about her or were laughing at the prank they had played. Her aunt told her she had "no social graces" instead of trying to understand how awkward social situations were for an autistic girl who had suffered multiple abandonments.

I would want my younger self to know that I now have a family I wouldn't trade for anything. I've made peace with my real mother and I have as much peace as I can with the ghost of my aunt. My "Spiritual Mom" still prays for me and encourages me; time has proved that friendship solid. I've connected with a group of writers who know that adoption is one of the most painful things anyone can go through, that some of the hurt can last a lifetime, but that it doesn't have to hurt every minute of every day. Not if you learn ways to fight the pain.

My younger self needed to be understood and validated. I still wish someone could have done that for her, or helped her do it for herself. My younger self and I, we're getting there now. Perhaps one of the most important lessons to accept is that nobody can go back in time and do things over.

TRACY AABEY-HAMMOND
ART

BROKEN HEART ADOPTION PENDANT
Medium: Sterling Silver

A HANDFUL OF BROKEN HEARTS
Medium: Sterling Silver

LEIGHA BASINI

ESSAY

A Different Life

ONCE SHE RETIRED, MY MOTHER moved to a Southern town with one traffic light and a sign that proudly says "Population 464." At dusk, hues of magenta and orange permeate the sky above a rolling cow pasture. Trees slowly dance in unison, and crickets sing to their swaying. Here, the rules are simple: doors are unlocked, shoes are optional, and banana bread is the cure for all troubles.

During wintertime visits, smoke pours endlessly out of chimneys— the only heat for many save for a blanket or human touch— and clusters of snow dreamily envelop the trees that a man will soon cut and load onto a truck, bound for the city Christmas tree lots. I sit by the fire with her friends, who under a thick layer of pan-cake makeup and big hair are disarmingly real. I pull out of her driveway, trying not to cry, as my car crunches over the gravel, the trees dotting the highway soon turning to familiar concrete walls.

I sent my mom an article explaining her county is the poorest in the state, whereas mine is the second richest in the nation. As I sat in my car, part of my nightly commute in a sea of seemingly parked cars, we chatted on the phone about the article.

"I know people couldn't get by if they didn't fish and hunt," she observed. "But we're resourceful and take care of each other." My mother runs the local food pantry and is the town's self-appointed den mother, finding people odd jobs and driving strangers to vote, even if for the wrong party.

The adoption agency promised my parents that I would have a better life than the one I would have had growing up on Jeju Island, not unlike the lives they created for themselves with the internal fortitude that comes from that generation. After all, 1970s Jeju was not rural America. Its poverty wasn't mom-and-pop stores with whitewashed porches and creaky rocking chairs. Jeju, with breadwinning *haenyeo* in wetsuits who held up the day's prize, wriggling in their wrinkled hands, held no trace of Norman Rockwell.

The local newspaper declared "one little Korean will someday be awfully glad" my parents adopted me. My father mused aloud to the journalist that I "wouldn't look good" diving for shellfish— I'd "make a better doctor, instead."

I doggedly pursued the American dream, my loving parents with me every step. The dream was just that— something of folklore and fairy tales— but I was determined to build this dream until it was so real that I could hold it in the palm of my hand, pull it from my pocket and feel its warmth radiate against my slender fingers. Success was not about money, it was about proving that my journey halfway around the world had greater meaning, that I deserved to exist. Though my family certainly never told me this or gave me any reason to believe it, the center of my unconscious saw a wadded up baby who had clung to the outermost fringes of the world, when a Godly stork swooped in and changed my fate.

Childhood playdates turned sour when I announced I was a doctor instead of a housewife when playing "house." Never mind that I could have delivered the mass of Cabbage Patch Kids stuffed under friends' shirts, the babies instead miraculously jumping out of stomachs. No one needed doctors inside the jumble of old sofa cushions and sheets that we called mansions.

Straight A's were expected, but by whom, I never asked. It was easiest to blame my parents. "They don't pay me to get good grades, they *expect* it," I would say to friends who brandished cold, hard cash for As, Bs, and even Cs. Being the only Asian kid made me an easy math club recruit, and with owl-like tortoiseshell glasses and a frizzy spiral perm that spread out past my shoulders, it was only a matter of time before I became a band geek and three-time spelling bee champ. I felt vaguely Eliza Doolittle when friends congratulated my parents.

Being the unwitting poster child for a successful adoption made setbacks devastating. I took a B+ test and sat at the kitchen desk, carefully tearing it into hundreds of pieces, tears falling on the bits and turning them to mush. Many days I refused to go to school altogether and would "forget" to change out of my pajamas or put on shoes. On mornings when I stood still as a Totem pole in the front yard, daring my parents to make me go to school, neighbors scattered into their houses like frightened mice when they hear someone approach. This mysterious fear of failure suffocated me, as inexplicably as the way I entered this world, perhaps plucked from a bush when a sad sprout of what could hardly be called hair indicated I was ripe.

"Patience, faith, reward," was my father's mantra. "When is the reward part?" I asked, wondering when I would finally be able to hold that elusive dream. I finished college two years early and joined the Asian students' club in law school, only to feel like a fraud as I fumbled with my chopsticks at Benihana, my eyes never moving from my plate.

I passed the bar. Check. Got a job. Check. Got married. Check. We honeymooned on a Pacific island in our own thatched-roof bungalow, where we decompressed to the tune of $1,000 a night.

Sitting behind a desk for ten hours a day, I knew how close I was. No matter that I had exchanged my art projects and cooking for a daily three-hour commute. In my head, the American dream – *my* American dream – was about to unfurl with banners to match.

"One little Korean will someday be awfully glad..."

It started out the way I had felt as a child when a tooth fell out, my tongue weaving between the two teeth flanking the gap, repetitively touching the smooth gum. What was this? The dizzying merry-go-round of life had never given me time to get off. I had perfected autopilot, and suddenly, an unknown voice was nibbling away at my perfect exterior.

"What was Korea like?" I asked my mother on a recent summertime visit, knowing the answer.

"Very, very poor," she said, as we picked plums from her yard by the dirt road. "You were so skinny."

"Right, I *was* skinny," I laughed as I wiped sweat on my forehead with the back of my hand. I had wanted to put the plums in clafoutis, but maybe I should just eat them raw, I thought.

Later, as we sampled heirloom tomatoes and pickled vegetables at the farmers' market that appears Saturday mornings next to the do-it-yourself car wash, she said, "It was so hot there. So humid. The air conditioning in the hotel was just this tiny hole in the ceiling. People hardly had enough to survive."

Soon after, my husband and I left for Korea, my hand gripping his as hard as I could as our plane took off. Jeju, once filled with dirt roads, rectangular houses made of lava rock and thatched roofs, and outhouses, is now a haven for vacationers in need of a break from the office. It is home to a Dunkin' Donuts, Ripley's Believe it or Not!, and a Hello Kitty museum. The houses were gone, except for an occasional one that serves as a garage. There was no trace of an outhouse; instead, I took videos of the multi-function electric toilets— thrones really worthy of royalty— to show friends at home. I swam with the *haenyeo* until I couldn't keep up and let my body melt into the ocean. I wondered if my own desperate tears had created this ocean that separated me from a Jeju that no longer seemed to exist.

We returned home, and I kept searching for that slice of existence, of what could have been. I happened on a 1970s video of a young girl in Jeju and watched it over and over, freezing each frame. I traced her face on the screen with my finger, a girl with rosy cheeks who washed the family clothes in a well fed with ocean water. She celebrated her grandfather's birthday with the village by removing her shoes before bowing and adding her gift next to a neat stack of apples. As she accompanied her mother to the neighborhood market, she smiled with a weightlessness that I have never known.

Today, we may both sip Dunkin Donuts coffee and daydream about mother-daughter days at the market. But I am not that girl. At family gatherings, she will reminisce about the hard times and how the family's strength pulled them out of poverty. And I will quietly wonder about a time and people I don't remember.

This winter, I will make snow angels in my mother's yard and pad around her house in my pajamas and slippers. We will celebrate old traditions and roast marshmallows outside until the fire calls us in. I will return home laden with gifts I don't need and resolutions I might keep— to love more, work less, and remember how the Jeju Ocean swaddled me in ethereal softness. I will return home.

ANNA CAVANAGH

ESSAY

Liberating Perspectives:
ACKNOWLEDGING THE REALITIES AND
EXPERIENCES OF ADOPTED PEOPLE

JUST AS FOR MANY OTHERS, the Flip the Script on adoption social media movement has helped me to validate my experiences and encouraged me to find my voice. Initially the Flip the Script on adoption movement was started as a response to the National Adoption Month by the Lost Daughters writing collective in November 2014.

National Adoption Month takes place every year in the United States and is aimed at raising awareness around adoption. However, sadly during this month, adoption stories are primarily told and dominated by adoptive parents and agencies, celebrating adoption as a selfless act and exclusively joyous event.

Yet, our adoptee voices are important and valid; only we can talk about how it feels to be adopted, including the joys, as well as the challenges of our experiences and of growing up with very limited or no knowledge of our origins.

Although I always knew I was adopted when I was growing up, it took me a long time to understand what it means and how it impacted me. I was born out of wedlock in 1985 in a Catholic town in Germany and (adopted out) relinquished a few days after my birth. There was not much openness around adoption at that time. All the information that my adoptive parents were given was to tell me that I was adopted from an early age on and to tell me that I could get a copy of my original birth certificate and search for my birth mother once I was 18 years old. They were also told to raise me "as if" I was their biological child.

As a consequence, when I was growing up, adoption or anything related to it was rarely discussed. I remember that we had one children's picture book at home that explained adoption and what it means. The book told the story of a happily married couple who unfortunately couldn't have children of their own. The book went on to describe how sad the couple was about that. To fulfill their wish to have children, the couple went to a home where a lot of children lived who didn't have a family. The couple chose the baby they liked best and the book ends with the family living happily ever after.

Reflecting on the book now and how it teaches children about adoption, it is impossible to overlook its inherent flaws and gaps. Adoptive children are not handpicked by adoptive parents as described in the book and the biological family of the adopted child is not mentioned once. It rather appears as if the biological mother and family do not play any role in the relinquishment process or later on in the adopted child's life, as if they are ghosts who do not exist.

Just as taught in the book, I learned very quickly it was better not to mention my biological mother or family and not to speak of myself as 'adopted'. It saddened my well-meaning and loving adoptive parents, especially my adoptive mother, if I did. They repeatedly told me that they did not think of me as "adopted" and that no one needed to know about that— I was "their" child. Even though that was well-intended, it was denying my truth.

The truth is that my adoptive parents did not create and give birth to me even though it is saying that on my birth certificate;

The truth is that growing up and not seeing myself reflected anywhere was incredibly isolating and confusing;

The truth is that I never forgot my birth mum; my body remembered her even if my mind did not;

The truth is that having loving adoptive parents did not negate the pain and grief of losing my entire biological family and ancestry.

The truth is that growing up without any knowledge of my origins made we sometimes wonder why I was born and alive at all.

The Flip the Script movement encouraged me to voice my truths. It is important that we continue to Flip the Script so that other adopted people can voice their diverse truths too. If we adopted people are silenced in the spaces that discuss adoption and only allowed to speak in words that portray it as a pain-free simple solution and entirely happy event, we run the danger of keeping our pain and grief inside.

To develop a new more comprehensive script that reflects adoption as a complex lifelong experience, is particularly important for the younger and new generations of adopted people and their families. By speaking out and flipping the script, we help pave the way for them. Hopefully by doing this and by developing a new more comprehensive script, we will stop them from being silent out of 'adoption loyalty' and will make it easier for them to find their voice, to talk openly and without guilt about the losses and grief they may have experienced and find healthy ways to process them.

Finding our voices can help us heal. It's time to diversify the adoption narrative; it's time to speak out and make our voices be heard.

"and when we speak we are afraid
our words will not be heard
nor welcomed
but when we are silent
we are still afraid
So it is better to speak"

-Audre Lorde

JAMIE LYNN

ART

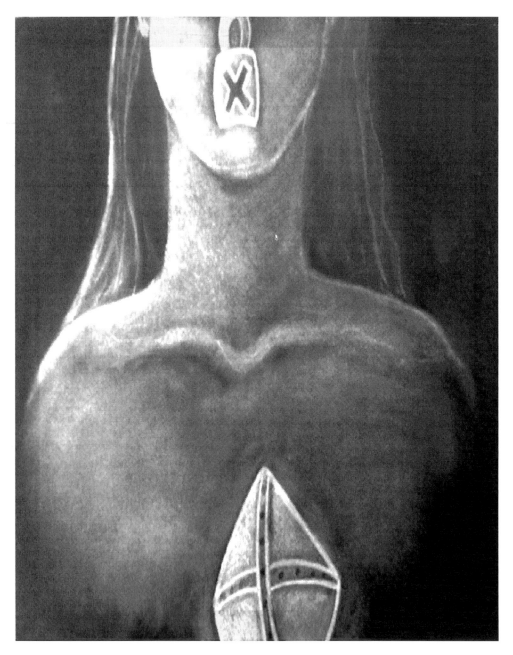

IMPOSED SILENCE

SOOJUNG JO

POETRY

Dissolution

I was meant to be a tree
bathed in soil and sun
coiling my finger branches through a drenching rain
while insects chewed my heart
and I burrowed deeper into the courageous land
Until we all
soil, sun, rain, insects
were one.
But a pigeon fought a war
with a dove
and carried my husked seed into the dry season
While I starved.
I was meant to be a gale
chopped into pounding beats
on a window sill
outside the families
who cowered from the chill of my howl.
But my path was hollow
and homeless
so I howled unfettered
and I met no one
until my wind faded to a place
where my force
Meant nothing.
I was meant to be a song
rising like a soul
toward a silver heaven
where the singular
Insular
light of my tone

made salvation for the lost.
But I was caught in the throat
of a man
who swallowed me in large bites
and then slept in his chair
till I dissipated
To breath.
I was meant to be a stone
heavy and dense,
rolled amongst the grasses
and worms
who held me like a daughter,
a mother, a sister.
But I was lifted
into the thieving pocket of a clever child,
held against her candies and fairytales,
Then painted as a pebble
and laid beside her playthings
until I become a relic
of a myth
and forgotten
Amongst the dust.

MATTHEW SALESSES

ESSAY

Post-Magical Thinking America

THIS SEMESTER, A STRANGE THING happened. A student came to my office hours to complain about the difficulties of understanding her own oppression.

I teach a course called "Asians in the Media" at the University of Houston, where I am a Ph.D. candidate in Literature and Creative Writing. The student is Asian American and has taken other courses in Asian American Studies. Her complaint was how hard it is on her to know that she is oppressed systematically by her country. She had it easier, she told me, before she knew that she was being marginalized. She expressed a wish to go back to not knowing. What could she do? She has a white boyfriend whom she wishes to marry. Why shouldn't she be able to become a doctor or lawyer and live out a sort of ignorance-is-bliss?

I found myself very much identifying with her desire, and empathizing with her fear of the world she now knows she lives in. Sometimes knowledge is a very difficult thing to deal with. As a teacher, I admitted to her, that difficulty is something we want—we want to complicate knowledge. And yet, I could understand the very real truth that perhaps her life would be happier if she didn't know that her country values her happiness less than certain other people's happiness.

I have been thinking about our conversation ever since. I have been thinking about how close the student seemed to a breakdown. I have been thinking about whether it indeed screws up her life to know about white supremacy. I have been thinking about how unhelpful it is to tell students that in a decade or so, they will appreciate having learned what they learned. I have been thinking about how unhelpful it is to tell students that they will live more fulfilled lives if they understand the system under which those lives are led. I don't know if that is even true.

I consider myself an expert in denial, as much of an expert as one can be solely from experience. I know too well that much of the ignorance my student desires to return to is closer to denial. It is denial when we can rattle off a list of times people have greeted us with "Ni hao" or asked where we are really from, and yet we claim not to "know" that the problem is systematic. Denial is not simple, and it is easier to achieve if we blame ourselves, if we do not have something larger to explain why we are under attack. When I was in my own denial about systematic racism, I understood micro-aggressions to be well-intentioned curiosity, and I understood my anxiety and shame to be a personal inability to accept the good intentions of white people. My discomfort was mine. Admitting what I knew would make the discomfort shared, systematic, but also larger than me and therefore uncontrollable—fixing oneself is less daunting than fixing a system.

For most of my life as a Korean adoptee with white parents and white friends, I lived with the kind of ignorance my student misses. And the fact is— I can indeed claim that I was happier then. I was happier when I believed adoption had nothing to do with supply and demand, war and colonialism. I was happier when I believed that if I dressed "properly" and spoke "properly" that I could escape being asked where I was really from. I was happier when I believed the story my parents had always told me: that anyone who works hard enough will find success. I believed the stereotypical immigrant American dream, even though that belief was married to a belief about white Americans.

I remember the doubts, of course, when people would call me Chink or monkey or tell me to go back to my country. But often the symptoms of systematic racism are so subtle that the cause is difficult to diagnose. The symptoms were losing friends seemingly for no reason. They were "positive" stereotypes. They were not getting playing time on the basketball court because I was "streaky" and my successes "came out of nowhere." They could be interpreted as misunderstandings or flukes or minor inconveniences... if only I believed they were. I was happier when I practiced magical thinking.

I took my first course in Asian American Studies as an undergrad—it was actually a literature course I have written about elsewhere. I mention that course because of how long it took me to figure out what I had learned from it. What makes awareness so hard sometimes is not the fact of waking up, but the years it takes to see that you are awake and that you can't go back to sleep. It can take years, too, to see that waking up is as much about seeing the system as it is about seeing one's place in it. For some, oppression will always be personal.

One of the first things to get my attention in the Asian American literature course was an "article" my professor brought in. The article was simply photos of Asian men with the tagline: "Gay or Asian?" We discussed the emasculation of Asian males. Incorporating this knowledge meant acknowledging that I was rarely seen as desirable. That acknowledgement, of course, did nothing to improve my self-esteem. However, it did tie my self-esteem to being Asian. A strange kind of progress.

I only saw a single symptom. My eyes did not open immediately. I raged against my emasculation at first, a personal, limiting rage. When the lack of Asians in the media came up, I raged against that too. When we got to sugar cane plantations, Japanese internment camps, the murder of Vincent Chin, I added and added to my anger. I felt unhappy, lost, and powerless. The year after, I went to Prague and hardly had a single conversation with another person of color.

Recently I was with a friend and his wife and she was talking about a Vietnamese American woman who gave her kids Anglo names. My friend's wife said that she would make sure to give their kids "Hispanic names." This recalled a conversation I'd had at a writing conference a few weeks earlier—a Vietnamese American writer mentioned that a white friend had said it was sad that the writer had given her kids Anglo names. It was stated as if the writer had somehow erased the kids' culture. The white friend decided it was up to her to police the writer's heritage. My friend's wife asked for my opinion. I said parents should be able to name their kids whatever they choose.

I could feel my friend's discomfort. About a year earlier, I wrote an article for Salon about a class we were in together, where a white student had wanted to police a Hispanic TV reporter's pronunciation of his own name, the same name as my friend's.

It is amazing how coincidental this all seems. How common these incidences are.

"This is why people in the program hate me," I joked.

My friend said people are afraid of saying the wrong thing around me.

"Good," I said. "I don't want them to say the wrong thing around me."

After he dropped me off, I thought about whether I meant what I had told him. What is the role of fear in equality? I've been afraid for most of my life to say the wrong thing, because I have been afraid that other people would say the wrong thing to me. I'm still consistently afraid of other people saying the wrong thing to me or about me. If I inspire fear of political incorrectness in others, then that saves me real pain. Perhaps that fear also means that the other person is aware that she might cause pain. Perhaps the resistance to policing political correctness is a desire to embrace denial. Aren't we afraid to say the wrong thing because we indeed have a sense of what the wrong thing is and a sense that we might say it?

About a year ago, I wrote an essay essentially stating that I was getting out of the "race beat," after another white killing of a black man. I had to stop writing reaction pieces because the news and opinion cycle began to seem weightless and ineffective. I would write about some tragedy, people would feel shared outrage, and then that tragedy would make way for a new tragedy and new outrage. What was the point of feeding the reaction machine? What was the point when real change means change to the system? What was the point when having a voice never felt like really having a voice?

In November I watched the #FliptheScript hashtag gain momentum and change the conversation. I saw anxiety in the media over the subject of adoption and whose voices are usually heard—as the country dealt with a rising awareness of minority voices in general. It makes me wonder. In the classroom, when I mention white supremacy or the colonization of the body, a few heads nod; more turn away in fear. Maybe I see hope in that fear. Fear of people's own complicity. Hope that adoptive parents who police adoptee's rights are afraid of their own increasing knowledge. Some people can see the truth and don't want to. The bells are ringing. What if this country is waking up?

MILA C. KONOMOS
POETRY

The Experiment

I.
 i vanished.

and.
i am vanishing.

as a secret
that remains untold,
that lies down with the dead,

as though it had never lived.

that it could be recruited
for the Great Experiment
to quench the thirst

of the Great White Hope.

who cannot feel
complete

without taking on a good deed
to love and to hold and to cherish
to mold and to form and to push

into their image
into their arms
into their calculated world of privilege

where everything and everyone is

Perfect.
Pristine.
For the Viewing—

Look at
my Little Black Doll.

Gawk at
my Golden China Doll.

Covet
these Beautiful Ethnic Children
behind these thin glass walls

With their mothers and fathers
brothers and sisters
grandmothers and grandfathers

weeping at their feet.

the Great White Light
will not see you

the Great White Trumpet
will not hear you

the Great White Wisdom

will take you.
away.
from it all.

Because you do not need what the Great White All
can not give.

Because you want what the Great White Almighty has.

It is Divine.
It is. My.
Mandate.

And it has the papers to prove it—
balled up in its fist.

You can not compete
with
the Law of Green and White.

By which all abide.

II.
 And now that it is too late
to retrieve
that
which was thrown away.

You are trapped.
Shoved.
Away.

like an embezzled jewel
in the corner of a
dark, locked
drawer.

And although it is never too late to.
submit to.
the Law of Green and White

will not.
get you out.
Not this time

it will not save you.
Not in this life.

For, do you not know, dear,

you have already been saved.

from the Person

the People
the Language
the Land
the Family
the Love

you might have been

nothing
no one

without us.

III.
 So be sure to fulfill your obligation
And utter with profusion
the gratitude

of being granted the mercy
of being permitted the opportunity
to be strapped down to the tails of its coat:

you are welcome,
my darling,

as long as you
silence the wailing lump

trying to escape from your precious little throat

where your insignificant
whining
impotent

voice resides

no one will listen to

you were just an
experiment,

just another subject,

statistic,

dot. on. a. line.
of the Great White Graph,

that the Great White World will choose to

dismiss,

will choose to
forget,

will lock in a box,

All for.

All in.

the only name that exists,

all hail, America,

all of you,
all of us,

everyone,

all in the sacred name.
of:

The Great White Love.

Two Tongues

I.

 I knew you once

like a fish knows water
like a bird knows sky

You took root
and sprouted

throbbing,
nascent,
erupting,
in the interstices
crackling with sound and a music
that

began to teach me
of love
and connection
family and
belonging
life and
world.

Until,
as if suddenly,
you went silent.
Dim.
Began to wither,
shrivel

until you turned brown and brittle
until you turned to dust
that eventually
was kicked away

blown away

into shadow that
became darkness
that became void

until

I lost you.

forever.

Like the severing of a tongue—

and you took
the love and
connection
the family and
belonging
the life and
the world

with you.

II.
You were replaced
by a more perfect love
and connection
a richer family
and belonging
a more meaningful life
and world

Your erasure was divine providence

Your beauty created to be defiled
Your music played to be interrupted
Your roots planted to be extricated

III.
I am calling you back

on my hands and knees
on my severed tongue

chiseling my way back to
the treasure
entombed

beneath a ceaseless precipice
of pain and weeping
wounding and healing
dangling and standing

one by one

i find these infinite
miniscule threads
flickering

these smoldering chemicals
barely lingering

where tragedy and triumph collide
loss and reclamation merge
sorrow and hope bond

this is the substrate
into which you will take hold

and I,
like a freak of overcoming,
will hold my two tongues

as they flap in your hot gales

like flags proclaiming

both my shame and my redemption
my lost and my found:

love and
connection
family and
belonging
life and
world.

I knew you once

like a baby knows her mother

a baby knows his mother

like a fish knows water
like a bird knows sky

like a

Baby.

Knows.

Her
Mother.

DIANE WHEATON

ESSAY

The Broken Box

I'VE ALWAYS KNOWN I WAS adopted. At five years old, I played with a little boy who was the same age, who was also adopted. I knew that because our mother's used to talk about us while we played. Several years later, I felt special being an adopted child because my parents told me they chose me out of many other children, like the hall in *Madeleine*, I suppose. A kind thing to say to an adopted child, but nothing could be more farther from the truth.

On a morning in late March 1956, my parents-to-be received a phone call from the county informing them of a baby girl available for adoption. We were a "good match" meaning I met their criteria through ethnicity, religion and desire. The social worker gave them limited information about my birth parents and then, after viewing me, as one who seeks a desired pet to love in a shelter, they said yes to parent a stranger's child.

They were not prepared for my homecoming. There was no pink baby shower with cake and happy gifts. No family and friends gathered to welcome my arrival. There were no clothes, diapers or crib.

After many years of trying and waiting, my parents had a baby. It must've been very exciting for them. I can only imagine the phone calls they made. I wish I knew how I reacted when they took me home. Was I scared leaving with strangers, but then, everyone was a stranger.

Sick and losing weight, the county had removed me from the foster home where I had been living the past two and a half months. It made me wonder if my foster mother ever rocked or comforted me.

As an infant, I didn't have the understanding, but I had the feelings. Whatever they were, they were raw and natural. Is this when the feelings of loss and loneliness began? The primal wound reared its ugly head for recognition and comfort, because the reality was, no one loved me deeply in the beginning. The familiar heartbeat that soothed me in utero was gone; forever. I was alone.

My parents were supposed to rescue me from the foster care system. Instead, they rescued themselves. They lost six babies of their own before they adopted me. Six. That is a lot of trying and despair to overcome. They never grieved their great loss and hope of having a child of their own before I came into their lives.

This tough World War II generation my parents were a member of, had already witnessed hardship and heartache in their young lives. They were a stalwart people, adept at burying grief and loss in order to get on with their lives.

Adoption was an answered prayer to their heartache. I had a big job ahead of me to try and make them happy. Being the savior child, they tried to mold me into someone I wasn't, so the reminder of our differentness wouldn't be so transparent. I don't think they ever saw me as the one in need; the one who needed rescuing the most.

As a teenager, I stretched my wings out into the world and tried different things. I was sassy and rolled my eyes. My parents' became angry at my independent behavior, convincing me I was selfish and ungrateful for all they had done. Disillusioned and disappointed, my parents' couldn't revel in their narcissistic mirror anymore. When they couldn't control me, they couldn't love me. Deep in my soul the familiar loss whispered, hauntingly, that somehow I wasn't good enough. And so began the spiral descent of one who became dethroned.

Growing up, adoption was a word that was not open for discussion. To my wounded mother, there was too much grief and pain associated with it. Her loss, her trauma, buried deep. My mother never asked me how I felt about being adopted or if I had any questions she might be able to help me with. Once I understood what the word adoptee meant, I knew I was different from my friends. The silent conclusion was that having an unknown mother must be bad, bad enough that we couldn't talk about it; therefore I must be bad too. Such is the error of this family secret.

With the exception of my younger adopted brother, John, I didn't grow up knowing another adoptee. John and I spoke only a few times in our lives about being adopted. The last time was when he was in his late teens. He told me he didn't want to talk about finding his birth mother anymore. He felt she obviously didn't want him, so he didn't want her.

I didn't feel the same way about my birth mother. I often wondered about her, sometimes looking up at the stars at night outside my bedroom window, dreaming of meeting her, which seemed impossible at that time, before anyone knew what a home computer or internet was. A fantasy mother and her story were created in my mind over the years to answer my question as to why she had to let me go.

Faire tales and stories of child orphans mesmerized me as a child; children alone in this world. The stories resonated deep within. Their happy endings gave comfort and hope enabling me to imagine that I, too, would one day be okay and not feel lonely.

I didn't suffer from the darkness of depression as a child, though its cloak of heaviness and the color of blue enveloped me more than a few times. When these moments came, I relied on my muse to rescue me. Like an angel, my muse knew when she was needed, to make me feel safe enough to express myself through drawing, writing stories and sad songs.

We all live between light and dark. All families have problems and secrets of some sort. As we lived our comfortable life, we hid our pain and angst. I became adept at pretending and a skilled people-pleaser. Being a sensitive child, able to empathize with others, I was drawn to those who hurt. Helping others made me feel good to be needed by people I cared about.

Most people know how they arrived in the world, and as children, love to hear their story. Not ever knowing your story is unsettling, unfair and can make one feel unreal. It's hard to find yourself in the mirror when there is no one looking back at you. We all have struggles and crosses to bear. We walk different paths seeking answers, searching for our passions, trying to find a reason for being.

Growing up in a home where the word adoption was considered a bad word, made it all the more difficult to find your equilibrium, your sense of self. Had my parents been able to be open about their feelings and fears, showing compassion and understanding towards my brother and me, our lives might have turned out differently.

My brother fought the same inner battles as many adoptees, and at twenty-five years old, my handsome, intelligent, sweet brother committed suicide. John had been my parent's golden child, the one who blindly followed their direction for his life. It's not my parents' fault John chose to do what he did. The ultimate price was already paid. He lived his short life torn between his need for belonging, fighting feelings of abandonment that caused him to deny his own self in order to win the love and approval of his parents. Adoption can be a complicated bag of pain.

Even though I was grateful to God for my rebellious nature that saved me, marrying my best friend and raising two wonderful children, I sometimes felt alone. It was lingering about, like a chasm in the earth, where you cover the entrance with large, bushy branches, but you know it's still there, this deep, dark gaping hole in the ground, just waiting for you to trip and fall inside.

Mid-life, I decided to search for my birth family, and found them. The dream I had as a child, looking up at the stars at night, came true. Meeting my birth mother, and finding out I have six siblings and ten cousins on my maternal side was unbelievable. A genealogy trail leads back ten generations from Nashville to Belfast. No longer do I feel I was born under a rock, I have history and roots, deep ones.

How do I define my adoption experience? Loneliness and sadness have attached themselves to my cells for life. It's who I am and my life experience. Most days I'm good, but once in a while, the old tapes of thinking I'm not good enough and feeling alone come back to haunt me. Now that I know the old thoughts, they are easier to let go of, letting them float by as if on a river. I'm also learning to love and accept myself, realizing I don't need to try to please people in order to gain their approval.

Being adopted has influenced my life, but being an adoptee hasn't always been my main focus. Adoption is a strong undercurrent, but in the end, it probably won't be the defining tide of my life, but rather will be seen as a gift I prevailed over. A gift that was given in a broken box. The broken box needed care and to be made strong again to house the gift. Once repaired and strong, with the gift safe inside, it was ready to be given again, this time wrapped in the most beautiful paper and ribbon one could find. That's how I see my life now; as a beautiful gift restored.

KIMBERLY MCKEE, PHD

ESSAY

화이팅 (Fighting!):
RECUPERATING THE KNOWLEDGE OF ADOPTEES

As my family gathered for Thanksgiving in autumn 2014 I was asked to participate in the broader #FliptheScript social media conversation on Detroit's FOX affiliate. It was an honor to be included with amazing adoptee activists including Aselefech Evans, Joy Messinger, Joy Lieberthal Rho, Amanda Transue-Woolston, and Kevin Haebeom Vollmers. These appearances coincided with various FOX affiliates' National Adoption Month (November) programming and represented a marked departure from traditional adoption coverage, which is far too often dominated by the voices of adoptive parents. More importantly, what stood out about my television appearance was the fact that I was not asked to discuss my personal adoption story. It was an exhilarating moment. To be asked to speak on my professional expertise is something that Adoption Studies scholars or adoption practitioners who are also adoptees are not always asked to do. The ability to do so without deploying the personal story is revolutionary.

The adoptee renaissance has arrived. No longer are adoptee voices relegated to the periphery, whereby they are *spoken for* or ignored as if their experiences are irrelevant. We are living in a cultural moment that will be remembered for shifting the adoption conversation. No longer will calls for humanitarian rescue be accepted as solely heartwarming stories. Instead, we hear adoptees ask— why are we not discussing family preservation? Or examining the ethics involved in adoption? We are also seeing adoptees rally for open access to records in the US and abroad.

Adoptees intervene in adoption conversations in multiple ways on the individual and collective levels. Engendering discussion and debate is central to what I do. My research dismantles stereotypes concerning the persistence of South Korea's engagement in transnational adoption, deconstructs the false dichotomy of the angry or happy adoptee, and locates adoptees into the histories of Asian America. This complements my teaching where I provide students a new lens to consider adoption. We make connections to broader issues including reproductive justice, legacies of colonization and imperialism, and understandings of who are considered "good" parents. My participation in the broader adoption community also reflects my commitment to shifting the traditional adoption narrative. By recognizing that activism takes on many different forms we can see how various members in the adoption constellation can work collectively to transform how we understand adoption in mainstream society.

ADOPTION IN THE IVORY TOWER

As adoptee voices come to the forefront in mainstream adoption conversations, I find myself considering my place in this cultural turn. As an adult Korean adoptee academic studying Korean transnational adoption and representations of female Asian adoptees in popular culture, my research is central to how I flip the script. My scholarship exposes the growth of what I term the transnational adoption industrial complex – the neocolonial, multi-million dollar industry that commodifies children's bodies. I critically interrogate the intersections of the macro- and micro-levels of adoption, disrupting the ways in which transnational adoption became naturalized as a humanitarian child-saving endeavor. Part of this work includes foregrounding the voices and activism of adult adoptees. By dismantling the singular notion of adoption as Christian American act of rescue, I am part of a growing movement in Adoption Studies that re-centers the experiences of adoptees and critically interrogates who adoption benefits.[i]

This investment to disentangle adoption from its historical roots as a mechanism to rescue children from poverty and place them into homes of wealth and love fuels my work in the classroom. In my course Introduction to Intercultural Competence and Communication, we explore the intersections of adoption and religion. Moving from the Orphan Train movement from 1854 to 1929 to Harry and Bertha Holt's adoption of eight mixed-race orphans and establishment of Holt Adoption Program, we end with a discussion of the rise of evangelical adoptions in the twenty-first century.[ii] Students reflect on their initial assumptions about adoption, consider the first person perspectives of adult adoptees, and conduct a holistic assessment of the adoption process. Regarding the latter, students investigate the corruption associated with twenty-first century adoption practices, learn about the re-homing of adoptees, and listen to adoptees discuss their lived experiences.[iii] After engaging with this material, students propose examples of culturally competent and/or ethical adoption practices.[iv] Their allyship with adoptees after one class period astounds me. Students firmly believe that adoptive parents should not expect gratefulness from their child for his/her adoption and prepare for what it means to raise a child of a different racial or ethnic background then themselves.

A similar reaction to adoption occurs in the classroom when I discuss the transracial, domestic adoptions of Native American children with students in my Diversity in the United States course. I historicize the Indian Adoption Project within the legacies of the Indian Boarding School Project.[v] Our discussion focuses on how mainstream Americans' understanding of Indigenous families and their ability to parent is extricably linked to legacies of colonialism and assimilationist practices. In many instances this is one of the few times students directly grapple with the intersections of adoption and economic, political, and social justice frameworks.

By shifting the conversation of adoption in the classroom, students are exposed to adoptees' activism. They confront questions adoptive parents and adoptees are routinely in dialogue with online and off-line. I encourage them to consider the implications of placing monetary value on children's bodies in various adoption-pricing schemes. My intentions are to spark critical engagement with questions concerning who may parent. Encountering these questions, students routinely ask, why are we not looking at the systemic reasons for why birth parents are not "qualified" or better positioned to maintain intact families.

FINDING MY VOICE: DISCUSSING ADOPTION IN THE PUBLIC SPHERE

And yet the political is personal. Not only do I desire to dismantle mainstream narratives of adoption from inside higher education, I also seek to reframe the debates in other facets of my life. Within my role as the Assistant Director/Secretary and Advisory Council member for KAAN (the Korean American Adoptee Adoptive Family Network), we work together to situate our annual conference as a site for multiple perspectives and ideas to be exchanged. Via our Facebook page, we share articles that challenge the paradigm of adoption as humanitarian rescue, advocate for birth parents' rights to parent, and foreground adoptees' various perspectives on adoption. KAAN centers adult adoptee voices even as topics may make other stakeholders, such as adoptive parents, uncomfortable. Working through our collective discomfort builds a stronger coalition that locates adoption within the reproductive justice movement, acknowledges the rights of birth parents, supports adoptees' access to their histories, and recognizes adoptees as speaking truth to power.

KAAN is only one avenue I employ to enact change in adoption conversations. Intellectual engagement concerning adoption cannot only occur within the Ivory Tower. Rather, it is through the dissemination of scholarly material to the public via online magazines such as *Gazillion Voices*, blogs, YouTube, and other media appearances. By circulating knowledge in multiple platforms and arenas, scholars engage in participatory learning. In sharing my research and personal experiences with the adoption process, I seek to intervene in generalizations that promulgate a singular adoptee narrative of happiness and gratefulness. Through complicating this existing narrative, we contribute to an expanding knowledge base of adoption's lifelong impact on members of the adoption constellation.

More broadly, the work I undertake personally and professionally locates transracial, transnational adoptees within broader conversations regarding communities of color.[vi] The adopted experience cannot be overlooked. This commitment joins other adoptees of color that continually situate their lived experiences within broader narratives. For example, Aselefech Evans cautions parents of Ethiopian adoptees that failure to recognize how processes of racialization operate in the US will negatively impact their ability to navigate the nation as black Americans.[vii] Lisa Marie Rollins also shares what it means to grow up as a Black girl in a white family on her website, *A Birth Project*.[viii] Similarly, Vietnamese, Korean and Chinese adoptees position themselves within broader histories of American military involvement in Asia and Asian American immigration to the US. The inclusion of adoptees reveals the overlapping histories of adoptees, persons of color, and diasporic communities within broader narratives of colonization, militarization, and imperialism.

CALL ME ANGRY, THAT'S OKAY

As someone in the public adoption sphere, I grapple with the reductive dichotomy of happiness and gratefulness versus anger and ungratefulness to label adoptees. If one is happy and grateful, they are also considered well-adjusted and, presumably, successful. Alternatively, those who positioned as angry and ungrateful are automatically stereotyped as maladjusted and a failure, professionally and personally. These generalizations divide the adoptee community and create competing groups – one that is deemed legitimate and worthy of space at the metaphorical table versus those marked as illegitimate, unworthy of attention. And yet these sweeping remarks construct adoptees within a black and white binary that fails to look at the nuances found within any community.

The label of anger is often attributed to individuals who interrogate adoption practices and advocate for ethical adoptions and family preservation. To be an adoptee whose work is enmeshed in adoption means that I am cast as angry. Due to this label, I often am asked intrusive questions concerning the feelings of my adoptive parents towards my work. I have been accused of wanting waiting children to languish in orphanages if international adoption is terminated. While none of these accusations make me jump for joy inside, I have realized that it is okay to be considered angry. And yet, why I am angry may surprise you.

I am angry that mainstream society historically framed adoption as an act of rescue. But I am also overjoyed when students in my classroom dig deeper and look at the systemic causes of adoption.

I am angry that my birth mother had limited options at the age of eighteen, which caused my relinquishment. I am angry that misinformation and mishandling of adoption files prevent so many adoptees from reunion. And yet I remain grateful that I had the opportunity for reunion because my adoption occurred during an era when a better documentation system (while not ethical) was implemented in South Korea.

I am angry that films like *The Drop Box* (2014) capitalize on an over sixty-year rhetoric of Christian Americanism that positions adoption as the only option and locates South Korea as a site where abandoned children will be left on the streets with little chance of survival. Yet I am grateful for activists in South Korea and the United States who support unwed mothers and call for family preservation and ethical adoptions.

If I am labeled angry because I critically engage the transnational adoption industrial complex and believe adoptees and birth mothers should be at the center of any conversations concerning adoption, I am comfortable with this categorization. The term angry should not be treated as a pejorative to make people uncomfortable or seek approval.

I reflect on these moments of anger to give you a better sense of why I do what I do. When you're in the thick of adoption as an adoptee and a scholar, it's hard to disentangle oneself. Where does the work end and my life begin? But it was clear to me that complacency is not an option. Without adoptees advocating for themselves alongside their allies, we will remain perpetual children, continually *spoken for*. To change the conversation means we must reinsert and recuperate our lost voices.

(ENDNOTES)

i   See Laura Briggs, *Somebody's Children: The Politics of Transracial and Transnational Adoption* (Durham: Duke University Press, 2012); Sara K. Dorow, *Transnational Adoption: A Cultural Economy of Race, Gender, and Kinship* (New York: New York University Press, 2006); Tobias Hübinette, "Disembedded and Free-floating Bodies Out-of-place and Out-of-control: Examining the Borderline Existence of Adopted Koreans," *Adoption & Culture: The Interdisciplinary Journal of the Alliance for the Study of Adoption and Culture* 1, no. 1 (2007); Eleana J. Kim, *Adopted Territory: Transnational Korean Adoptees and the Politics of Belonging* (Durham: Duke University Press, 2010); and Kim Park Nelson, ""Loss Is More Than Sadness": Reading Dissent in Transracial Adoption Melodrama in The Language of Blood and First Person Plural," *Adoption and Culture* 1, no. 1 (2007). For a critique of the American domestic adoption market, see: Mirah Riben, *The Stork Market: America's Multi-billion Dollar Unregulated Adoption Industry* (Dayton: Advocate Publications, 2007).

ii   See Linda Gordon, *The Great Arizona Orphan Abduction* (Cambridge: Harvard University Press, 1999); Bertha Holt and David Wisner, *The Seed from the East* (Los Angeles: Oxford Press, 1956); and SooJin Pate, *From Orphan to Adoptee: U.S. Empire and Genealogies of Korean Adoption* (Minneapolis: University of Minnesota Press, 2014).

iii   See Kathryn Joyce, *The Child Catchers: Rescue, Trafficking, and the New Gospel of Adoption* (New York: PublicAffairs, 2013); Kathryn Joyce, "'The Child Catchers': Evangelicals and the Fake-Orphan Racket," The Daily Beast, April 24, 2013, accessed May 06, 2015, http://www.thedailybeast.com/witw/articles/2013/04/24/kathryn-joyce-s-the-child-catchers-inside-the-shadowy-world-of-adoption-trafficking.html; and Megan Twohey, "Reuters Investigates," Reuters, September 9, 2013, accessed May 06, 2015, http://www.reuters.com/investigates/adoption/#article/part1.

iv   Kimberly McKee, "Controlling Our Reproductive Destiny: Rethinking Adoption as the Better Option," Gazillion Voices Magazine, June 9, 2014, accessed May 06, 2015, http://gazillionvoices.com/controlling-our-reproductive-destiny-rethinking-adoption-as-the-better-option/#.U6GhaC-T69F.

v   See Heidi Kiiwetinepinesiik Stark and Kekek Jason Todd Stark, "Flying the Coop: ICWA and the Welfare of Indian Children," in *Outsiders Within: Writings on Transracial Adoption*, ed. Jane Jeong Trenka, Julia Chinyere Oparah, and Sun Yung Shin (South End Press: Cambridge, 2006); Adoptees Have Answers, "Adoptees Have Answers: Sandy White Hawk," YouTube, April 7, 2010, accessed May 06, 2015, https://www.youtube.com/watch?v=ZH-BHvACYiw; and Anna Bressanin and Ilya Shnitser, "Native Americans Recall Era of Forced Adoptions - BBC News," BBC News, November 21, 2012, accessed May 06, 2015, http://www.bbc.com/news/world-us-canada-20404764.

vi   See Kimberly McKee, "Tracing Our Histories: Making Connections between Adoption and Ethnic Studies," Gazillion Voices Magazine, December 2014, section goes here, accessed May 06, 2015, http://gazillionvoices.com/tracing-our-histories/#.VIXWuGTF9sB.

vii   Aselefech Evans, "Reflections on Ferguson, and on Raising Black Children," November 25, 2014, accessed May 6, 2015, http://www.thelostdaughters.com/2014/11/reflections-on-ferguson-and-on-raising.html.

viii   Lisa Marie Rollins, A Birth Project, 2005, accessed May 06, 2015, https://birthproject.wordpress.com/

BEATA SKONECKI, LMSW

ESSAY

Many Kinds Of Love

IT IS JANUARY 4; OUTSIDE rain lightly falls. But in my heart I am in Rzeszów and it is May and the city is blooming with color. The fields, grass, and meadows are lush and green. The poppies and orchids bud and slowly, tentatively, begin to unfurl after a long, harsh winter. Families stroll down the streets, chatting and laughing, absorbing the Sun's new and almost foreign warmth. The city is bursting and so is my heart; the love that surrounds me threatens to spill over.

For adoptees, home can be a very strange concept.

Being adopted, I have found, means being familiar with many different kinds of love, many varieties of connection. It's a roller-coaster of sorts. There's an immense amount of gratitude; yet an overarching sense of loss persists, and permeates every interaction, every decision, and every relationship.

But we are not always allowed to acknowledge this loss. We are told to be thankful, as though grief and gratitude cannot coexist.

I was born in Rzeszów, Poland, in July 1991. My mother had just turned fifteen years old, and her parents made the decision to place me in the local orphanage. My birth mother, upon leaving the hospital, went to town to try to gather details about my whereabouts. They could tell her nothing. The records were sealed.

Growing up, I always knew I was adopted. It was not a big deal and certainly not a secret. My parents were very open about our family story, and supportive of my attempting to reach out to my birth mother once I was an adult. I began to do as much research as I could on my own. I do not know much Polish— although I'm learning— and had little information to work with. I started by searching my birth last name. There were not many results. I was disappointed, but I kept trying. I posted in Polish-American forums. I joined genealogy websites. I was hungry for answers. I wanted to know where I came from.

Then I found a man with my last name on Facebook. And he lived in Rzeszów. Could this be a connection? I messaged him. I waited. I waited. Quite frankly, I had forgotten about the message altogether when, almost a year later, I received a reply.

The message was long and completely in Polish. I scanned through quickly and read: She mentioned the hospital I was born in, and the date I was born. It all matched up. "I have been waiting for this moment for 21 years," she wrote. She had had no idea where I was; if I was alive or dead.

The person I had messaged was her son, my biological brother.

I printed out the letter and ran outside to my dad, whose native language is Polish. It was a warm spring day and he was engrossed in yard work. I pushed the note towards him. "Dad, read this. Please. I think it's my birth mother. I really think it's her." My father abandoned his project, went inside, sat on the couch, and read the note. I watched his eyes dart back and forth.

"What does it say?" I inquired eagerly. My dad looked at me. I saw him quickly wipe a tear from his eye before he said, "This is it. This is her."

I'm going to meet her in 28 days.

This upcoming reunion, I've found, has yielded mixed reactions from extended family, acquaintances, and anyone who feels I would benefit from their opinion.

A few weeks ago, someone overheard my conversation and remarked, "Oh, you're meeting your birth mother? How nice." I thanked her. Then she proceeded with, "So where is your mom now?" Confused, I replied, "Well, she's home right now..." The woman interrupted, "Well after you meet your birth mother, will she still be your mom?"

How does one respond to a question like that?

A memory from when I was around eight years old resurfaces. "Where's your real mom?" my friend questioned. "She's in the kitchen," I replied, knowing my mom was preparing one of her incredible home-cooked meals. "No, I mean your real mom," she pushed on. I was getting annoyed. "I just told you. She's in the kitchen."

I cannot remember a time when I perceived one mom as more important than the other, one as more loving, and one as more "real." And I never will.

My birth mother brought me into this world, and my Mom taught me to read, took me to more doctors' appointments than I could ever count, and helped me with math homework for endless hours. My birth mother gave so many of her characteristics: her dark, wavy, thick hair, her green eyes, her love of singing and reading books. My Mom— and Dad— raised me. They encouraged me to go to college, and then grad school.

My mom taught me to self-advocate, and, through her example, how to be the source of gentle support and strength. My Mom's love is a soothing cup of tea after a long day; tender warmth that I knew I could rely on. And 4,000 miles away, my birth mother would message me: "I'm sorry I could not raise you." And almost every day: "I am so sad that I cannot hug you right now."

To attempt to compare their love is impossible.

My excitement over the prospect of meeting my birth mother has nothing to do with a supposed lack of love or support from my adoptive family. My love for my birth mother does not detract from or negate my love for my adoptive mom.

My thirst and quest for knowledge, for answers, to know more, to know why— has persisted since I was a small child. Seeking my family history and my roots are no different.

Every relationship is complex; to describe one of my mothers as "real" and not the other does a disservice to both their and my experiences.

There are many kinds of love. And they are all as real, valid, and beautiful as the next

NICOLE J. BURTON

ESSAY

Taking Charge Of "Adoptee"

F LIPPING THE SCRIPT ON THE term "adoptee" has my support one hundred and eighty degrees. We're children only a very short time, and adults for sixty, seventy, eighty years, living with a complex family situation entirely not of our making. I've come full circle on the term "adoptee." At first as a child growing up in Great Britain, I begrudgingly accepted that "adoptee" was what I was. It wasn't a widely-used term; "adopted" was more common. "I'm adopted." "She's adopted." "Why were you adopted?"

My adoptive parents were progressive for their era, telling me almost everything they knew about the circumstances of my birth and letting me see my adoption documents. I knew that my birthfather was a Jewish businessman, my mother was an artist, and that religion and his dark olive skin were the main reasons they couldn't marry in provincial England in 1956. I knew my birthmother's name and the name she gave me, Pippa. Since Pippa is the common diminutive of "Phillipa" in England, I grew up believing that my father's name was Philip and that she named me after him.

These facts turned out to be true when I searched and found my birthparents. The only omission was that my adoptive mother had known my birthfather's full name all along. She could have opened up my adoption at any time, except that in the 1960's, one didn't do such a thing. That would have been unheard of and completely unsupported, so I wasn't able to meet him till the mid 1980's when my adoptive mother spilled the beans and I searched and found him.

I began using the term "adopted person" after my memoir, *Swimming Up the Sun,* came out in 2008. As a writer and linguist, I blanched at the passive, powerless structure of the wimpy word, "adoptee." "I am an adopted person," I said.

"Refugee," "payee," "deportee," "adoptee." In English, the –ee suffix on a word means, literally, "an individual or object who is *acted upon.* The object of another's power. Passive receiver of services." I felt that "adoptee" encouraged others to see us as objects in a vast power system, wards of the State, perennial children. True, I *was* once an object, removed from one mother deemed by society as "illegitimate" because she was single, sexual, and working class, and given to another, properly married woman with a husband and middle-class prospects. Until England gave adult adoptees the right to get our own original birth certificates and adoption records in 1975 (forty years ago and nothing bad has happened), I couldn't even access my own paperwork. That's powerless.

Yet after years in the adoption reform movement ("Why does adoption need to be reformed?" people ask), I've come to reclaim the term "adoptee." It is who we were and who we are now, and it's an easy way to identify ourselves as a worldwide tribe. Our diverse stories—whether international or domestic, transracial, raised in single parent, two parent, or blended families, of single or multiple ethnicities—grow out of similar conditions: in most cases, our mothers were not allowed to be our mothers. They were poor or single or both. They were coerced into surrendering us, overtly or covertly. Resources were applied to break up our families rather than try to preserve them. Some of us were outright stolen; some were traded, bought and sold. None of us adopted as babies or young children had a voice in where we went or with whom we ended up. We *were* objects. Commodities. "Trafficked" is an appropriate term.

Yet, we were every one of us born of mothers and fathers, and in many cases we were beloved. This is the way of human nature, the hard-wiring of human parents. As adults, we are free, self regulating, and deserving of full human rights, and the same right to associate that non-adoptees enjoy every day.

I hope to live to see the day when adoption is virtually extinct. I call myself an "adoption abolitionist." Though there will always be a handful of cases in which babies and children need new safe and loving homes, and where relatives and community members can't or won't provide such homes. In these cases, I say, "Bring on the strangers!" But never should any adoption or any assisted reproductive technique that results in a human being involve *anonymity* after the affected person becomes an adult. Never should that person be denied access to their original family. Agencies should be required to gather and maintain adoptee data and contact information. To know one's people is a fundamental human right. Policies, laws, trade, regulations, or the lack thereof that denies adoptees access to our biological kin is an up-and-down human rights violation.

We deserve the right to search and the necessary support to reunite with our biological kin, if we choose, free of regulation, stigma, or retribution. The barriers adoptees face in reconnecting with kin must come down. Laws must change. Societies must change and cease punishing women and the poor. To deny the rich treasure of what we, the approximately five million adoptees in America, have to offer the world is to stand on the wrong side of history. It's time for adoptees to Flip the Script.

THERE IS NO PLACE LIKE HOME
Medium: Screen Print in B/W & Color

ELIZABETH COLE
ESSAY

Being Real

WHEN I WAS AN INFANT something was taken from me without my permission. Of course, I don't remember it. I can imagine that my birth mom was in that hospital with me but mostly what feels real is that my adoptive family picked me up there, 5 weeks later.

Imagining is a big part of the adoption experience. One doesn't remember being an infant, what it was like to feel the empty space where our mothers were supposed to be. We know only that loss was sewn into our body and soul that day, and will remain as long as we do. We imagine that day, that woman, that loss, that mother. We imagine reaching out to her to stop her from walking away. We imagine her face and her life and her voice and her laugh. When I was growing up I pictured someone beautiful and famous. But the thing is, that is not a real mother. A movie star is a fantasy, not a real woman.

When I met my mother I felt real things. Fear and desire. Wanting and needing her, but an instinct to protect myself from her too. Looking at her there, for the first time, with khaki pants on. With her brown hair pulled back in clips. With an odd rendition of my smile. This was not a movie star— but a real person.

Getting to know her I found that she is as real and human and limited as my adoptive mom. In very different ways of course. She thinks gay marriage should be illegal? The movie star in my imagination most certainly did not think THAT. She is so buried in shame and religion that she is behind a wall I can never truly get through? She has had other very real problems in her life, like her husband being terminally ill for 6 years? She told me once she can't remember the details around my birth— that it feels like a book she once read? No I didn't imagine any of these things. Without realizing it, I had only imagined goodness, warmth, and beauty. Someone who would think exactly like me— only somehow better.

I wish I had a happy ending to offer. That I had suffered but learned and grew and eventually found a way to accept the real mothers I have, flaws and all. Logically I have no problem with their flaws, with them having different viewpoints than me, even with the adoption itself. No problem at all.

But this isn't about logic, is it? Logic would tell an alcoholic to stop drinking or a person with an eating disorder to be healthier. Being human is more than logic. It is being born, through great suffering and blood and milk and heavy breasts to drink from and the sex that caused you to be conceived. None of this is sterile or logical.

We are human, just like everyone else. No one expected us to be. They thought we just showed up in a blanket at a hospital or adoption agency or police station. They thought we could be molded by them, to be happy or appreciative of a better life. And logically I see how this could make sense and put someone's mind at ease.

But we must claim our humanity. We must be recognized as someone who was born. I want them to hear my mother scream, to see her legs pushed apart and her 16-year-old vagina gape shockingly to let me into the world and make me a real person. A real girl. I want them to see her and my birthfather, outside in the grass, awkwardly but passionately doing something a 14- and 15-year-old in our culture were not supposed to be doing. But they did it anyway because they were human and stupid and hormonal and rebellious and careless and carefree. Seeing my adoptive parents in their smart, fashionable clothes, ages 35 and 42, holding a little package... there is good in that, but it is not the same, can't anyone see how different that is? Where is the humanity in that? How do I become real and human when that is all anyone sees or acknowledges?

It is not to blame others that we speak, that we claim, that we push for understanding and acknowledgement. It never has been. People thinking that it's about blame are just another way to deny us in favor of our parents. That's who they sympathize with. Those are the "real" people with the smart clothes there. You might make them feel bad with all that talk about blood and vaginas. They might feel threatened or hurt. But if we don't push that bright red line of gratitude, then we accept that we are not human. Never were we born, we did not come from anywhere.

All this talk about what is real and what is not real. It's important. When I was 18 I gave birth to my own little boy, and I gave him away too. I had believed I was a ghost. I had believed in the fairy tale of non-humanness that made everyone so comfortable and nice. I was not expected to love fiercely, to demand help in a crisis, to claim anything or anyone as mine. I did not allow myself to claim his curly blond hair. Or his birth. Or his life. Or his love for his mother. I thought that I could be something other than human. But I can't. Try not eating or drinking or using the bathroom.

You can't do it and still live.

On the day that you decide you are not human and stop eating... you will begin to die.

I can't go back to that day and explain this to my 18 year-old self and take my baby home. But I can tell you— and I can insist that others hear it too. It's uncomfortable and painful and the reality makes me feel achingly vulnerable.

But I want to live.

I think all of us deserve to live.

And so we must.

ROSITA GONZALÉZ
Art

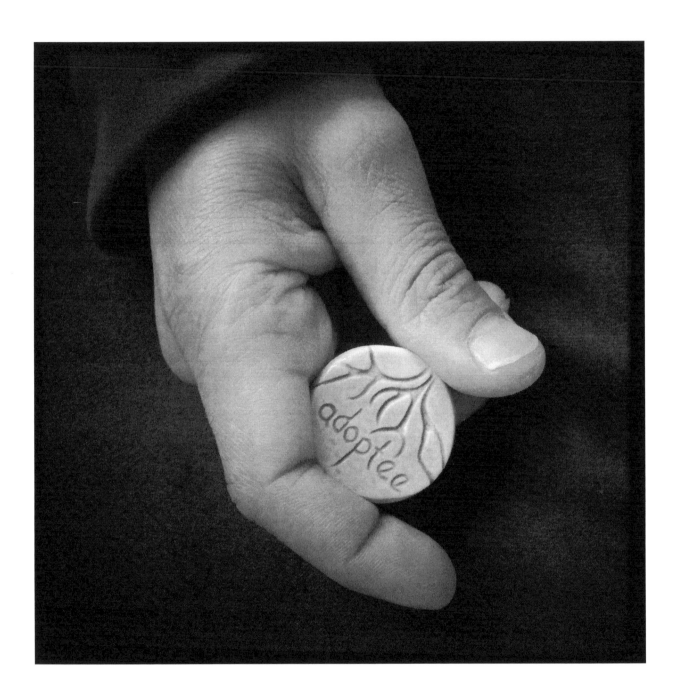

New Titles, New Stories

A S A CHILD, THE LIBRARY was one of my favorite places. I loved the endless adventures at my fingertips. There was something comforting, and also exciting, about knowing that anything I could ever want to know, and much which existed beyond my imagination, could be easily found amongst the library shelves. I devoured the stories from history, from authors' imaginations, and those constructed from the current world we live in.

Naturally, when I wanted to know about people like me, adoptees, I went to those trusted library shelves. But this visit was different. Unlike the many successes of the past, this time I found no comfort within those shelves. My hunger was left un-satiated. Diligent searches up and down the stacks left me empty handed and dejected. I searched the library aisles— adventure, history, and science fiction lined the shelves. Books filled the building from wall to wall, but the fact was that reflections of me, as an adoptee, were nowhere to be found.

"At least my mother loved me and didn't put me up for adoption!"

-Accusation of a friend in elementary school

It was the early 1990s and while social workers and clinicians were researching adoptee outcomes and interviewing parents about their children's adjustment, these research papers, journal articles, and limited monographs didn't make it to the shelves of my public library branch. Perhaps this was for the better. After all, I was not in search of clinical absolution but rather connection to others with similar life stories. Like many others, I grew up in a neighborhood where very few looked like me, and unlike some others, I did not grow up participating in adoptive family groups or culture camps. Instead, adoptee was wholly a solitary state of being. Like any other only (l)on(e)ly child, I found ways to entertain myself. My imagination created new worlds and spell-binding adventures. I unearthed scientific discoveries and provided answers for who I was and how my family made sense.

"You guys know about vampires?" Diaz asked.
"You know, vampires have no reflections in a mirror? There's this idea that monsters
don't have reflections in a mirror. And what I've always thought isn't that monsters
don't have reflections in a mirror. It's that if you want to make a human being into
a monster, deny them, at the cultural level, any reflection of themselves.

And growing up, I felt like a monster in some ways. I didn't see myself reflected at all.
I was like, "Yo, is something wrong with me?
That the whole society seems to think that people like me don't exist?

And part of what inspired me, was this deep desire that before I died, I would make
a couple of mirrors. That I would make some mirrors so that kids like me might
see themselves reflected back and might not feel so monstrous for it."

-Junot Díaz, Pulitzer-prize Winning Author

I had no idea that though I consistently felt isolated, I was far from an anomaly. Internationally there were others adapting to another country and culture. Nationally there were others assimilating to Whiteness yet integrating into homogeneous (White) communities. Even in my own city, there were others navigating the Black-White color line in a city that was still very much reaping the consequences of being the place of Martin Luther King, Jr.'s assassination while also negotiating the mores and values of the Bible Belt. Even though I did not know my connection to the broader transnational transracial adoption phenomenon, I would learn that others knew enough— enough to make conclusions (about how we've fared), enough to make decisions (about how much we need to know), and enough to make declarations (about who we are).

"She was giving me advice [about how to care for an infant], but I mean what
does she know. She doesn't have kids of her own. They were adopted."

-Reflection of a friend in undergrad regarding her mother-in-law

While others felt confident enough to make such allegations, publicly and privately with vast affects, their conclusions lacked comprehensive evidence. To be sure— I am adopted and this has had deep consequences; consequences which go well beyond outcomes and adjustment. But, I am much more than suspended moments in time or transgressions of U.S. conceptions of family-making and kinship ties. Yes, I am an adoptee (and yes, I am an American), but adoptee is more than static measurements or a categorization, something to be assessed, reported, and then filed away. It means to come to terms with being a representation for your experience, for what it means to be racialized in a certain way, what it means to create love and family and care beyond blood and with people who don't look like you, what it means to challenge these U.S. borders. It means being at peace with being marked— as othered because of your family construction and your supposed phenotype-culture mismatch— yet invisible— because of your race within U.S. racial hierarchy— and taking the awareness of both and being seen. Asserting yourSELF. Demanding to be seen.

Silence kills the soul;
it diminishes its possibilities to rise and fly and explore.
Silence withers what makes you human. The soul shrinks,
until it's nothing.

-Marlon Riggs, Filmmaker and Gay Rights Activist

It does not mean, however, that I acquiesce to external definitions about how I have come to be or ways that I should feel about where I am, neither where I am in this country, nor where I am in this family. Quite the contrary, it means I don't have to fit into the dominant adoptee narrative. It's an acknowledgement that I am always being defined— orphan, unwanted, unloved, loved, grateful, rescued, white, culture-less ... and always being seen through the lens of others' relationships to their family. People project their feelings about family relations and family making onto my family's formation. Yes, what onlookers say about adoption and how I should feel is directly related to their own family issues. They tell stories about me to bolster what they think about themselves, wish to be true about themselves, or what matches with their own values.

But just the same— I have my own stories to tell.

Sharing your story is also freedom-work. In storytelling, we are reminded
that we're not alone, that we are loved, & that love is work, too.

-Deray McKesson, Activist and Social Movement Curator

The stories I tell go far beyond the boundaries of the adoptee. Adoption is more than just an act — the act of abandonment, desire for a 'better' future, new family, new home, and new country. It is action. It is deconstructing, redefining, rearticulating.

It is better imagined Adoptee-American.

It is a politicized, racialized, historically-situated, and power-relation laden identity. We bear the marks of imperialism, colorism, colorblindness, commodification, and consumerism. Accepted individually but rejected collectively within the American imaginary of what is American. And, so the label adoptee, infantilizing and marginalizing, is insufficient in describing a full-grown, fully functioning, free standing collectivity who share a history, an upbringing, an experience and daily lived experiences, and who use those commonalities as a basis for community building, political platform, and advocacy.

Nobody's going to save you.
No one's going to cut you down, cut the thorns thick around you. No one's going to
storm the castle walls nor kiss awake your birth, climb down your hair, nor mount
you onto the white steed. There is no one who will feed the yearning.
Face it.
You will have to do,
do it yourself.

-Gloria E. Anzaldúa, Author and Theorist

We have both the right and the responsibility of telling our story. If we don't, then it will be told for us as it has been told for us for many years. Our stories are so much more complex than tropes about humanitarianism, Christian duty, Western superiority, those 'fit' to be parents, and how adoptees should feel about being adopted. Family is so much more complicated and nuanced than linear explanations. While narratives about helplessness and rescue are seductive to our American minds, they are flawed like the title 'adoptee,' inaccurate, misleading, and minimizing of our actual lived experiences. While the title adoptee does describe a part of me, I am not encapsulated within it. As with any title that is externally created and imposed, it must be negotiated. This could be acceptance of the term and how it is used by others, by those in power. It could be a rejection of the title in whole or in part, and the rejection could be active, rejecting and replacing or redefining, or it could be passive, rejecting and ignoring, believing because it does not matter to you or wholly define you that it is free of consequences. However, individual beliefs by themselves do not dismantle institutionally embedded tags. And so the collective movement to #FliptheScript is necessary. And while these social media declarations may influence what the public, prospective and current adoptive parents, social workers, and others think, it is not for them that we do this. It is for us. It is our story to tell.

CATHERINE A. JOHNSTON

ESSAY

Adopted. Adoptee. Adopting.

I OFTEN READ ESSAYS BY ADOPTEES who are parents sharing how grounding and affirming it is to see themselves mirrored in their children by birth, how powerful it is to finally have that biological connection. I understand that sentiment but it has never resonated for me. I always imagined that I would adopt a child. I think many adoptees think about adopting at some point— perhaps it is a way to return the 'favor' of our own adoptions, to pay it forward as a tangible act of gratitude, or as subconscious way to work out our own stuff. It was certainly all of that for me.

Until I actually became an adoptee... parenting an adoptee.

When I first met my husband-to-be we agreed on most parenting topics— how many kids (one), why we wanted a small family (overpopulation, ecological concerns, nervousness about being parents), our feeling about assisted reproduction (no, never). What we did not initially agree on was the possibility of adoption. He was unfamiliar with adoption, only knew one or two adoptees before me, and came from a family and culture (he is first generation Chinese American) that does not embrace adoption.

Adoption was really all I knew. My family included two kids, my brother and I, both of us adopted. When my parents divorced, my mother later married a man who had two sons, both adoptees, so now we were a family of six, all unrelated by birth. It was strangely comforting that we all shared *not* sharing anything. My primary family experiences did not involve biological connections, pregnancy or babies. I thought adoption was just normal.

When my husband and I married we gave the traditional baby-making route a solid effort. I was already 42 so we knew that the odds of pregnancy were slim. Though it was hard for me to sit with adoption being our second choice— it hit far too close to home— I respected my husband's preference to first try for a biological child and thought pregnancy would surely be a less complicated path to parenthood.

As we set out to become pregnant I became terrified. This went beyond the typical fear that I imagine most prospective new parents have. The hard truth was that I was simply afraid of having a biological child— a child that looked like me, that was part of me, that might prove love for biological children really is stronger than love for anyone else. What if my carefully constructed sense of self crumbled? What if everything I knew about families was wrong?

When I was very young being adopted made me special. That was the narrative back in my day. Other kids came out of their mother's bellies; I, however, was 'specially chosen'. I was wanted, selected, pick of the litter. I used to imagine a big grocery store where, instead of cans and boxes, the shelves were lined with babies in baskets. Prospective parents came in and picked out the prettiest babies and paid for them at the cash register. My six-year-old vision of adoption wasn't accurate or nuanced, but it made me feel unique and proud. For a child it was a powerful narrative — and for this kid growing up with divorced parents, remarriages, alcoholism and emotional abuse sometimes it was the only thing propping up my self-esteem.

In my teens, with yet another new stepfather, the new stepbrothers, and a heightened level of domestic dysfunction, adoption took on a new role for me. Being an adoptee gave me the emotional strength to separate from the daily misery of my family life. Because I had no genetic connection to any of the family I lived with I imagined I could somehow remain unscathed by their craziness. My new and improved personal adoption narrative was less about being special and more about being independent, self-sufficient and detached. Adoption became my protective shield.

During my early adult years my thinking about all things adoption became much more nuanced. I became acutely aware of my own fertility. Through hard personal experiences of becoming pregnant and deciding not to carry the children to term, I learned about choice, the limits of gratitude, and perpetuating cycles of dysfunction. I developed a deep empathy for what my birthmother likely went through when she was pregnant with me. During this time of my life I met my birth mother. It was and wasn't everything I had imagined it would be. It was profound to finally see myself in another person yet also sobering to realize that much of my life story mirrored hers. It turned out that being adopted wasn't really a free pass from intergenerational dysfunction after all.

As my husband and I moved onto plan B, I was secretly relieved. Given that adopting was always my first choice and I wasn't infertile, at least not historically, this plan B was really more of a win-win than a consolation prize. And with all of my lived experiences I was an adoption expert, wasn't I? This would be easy. I already knew the script.

The process of adopting our child, however, was a revelation. Up until this moment adoption had always been a personal thing— my story, my life. Now I found myself involved with the business of adoption, dealing with paperwork, financial statements, perfunctory adoption education classes, and a long schedule of payments and fees. The entire process was strangely impersonal.

While we waited for our future child, I joined internet groups and forums and did vast amounts of reading. I learned about the history of adoption, colonialism, coercion, systematic corruption, market economics and trafficking. I discovered adoptee blogs where stories mirrored my own experiences. I joined adoptive parent internet forums where my perspective as an adoptee, an adult who had lived through adoption, was constantly dismissed. I joined adult adoptee spaces where being an adoptive parent was vilified. Most painful were encounters with adult adoptees that refused to engage with me as a peer once they learned I was also becoming an adoptive parent.

My misgivings were huge. I realized that we had become participants in system that was not only flawed but often unethical. Sadly, my childhood vision of a baby store wasn't all that far from reality. Angry, confused, betrayed, overwhelmed— to say I was deeply conflicted is an understatement.

When we received the call from our adoption agency telling us we had been matched with a baby girl it got real. This adoption, this child— it had to be a new story for both of us. I took responsibility for the choices I had made as the adopter but there was just no room for guilt and remorse about participating in a system that I no longer believed in. I needed to parent with intention and integrity in order to dismantle this pervasive legacy of adoption that had affected both me and this child we were soon to meet. This little girl was more than my daughter; she was one of my tribe. Being adopted would be the norm, but unlike when I was growing up, our family would focus on what it means to be adopted from the adoptee perspective rather than what it means from the adoptive parent perspective. I hoped that an adoptee consciously parenting another adoptee could be a small act of rebellion.

It has not always been easy. Hearing my daughter's cries of grief for what she had lost (her mother, her foster mother, everything that she knew) almost broke me. I've stumbled in talking to her about her story and have been tempted to pretty up the details to make it easier to say and easier to hear. And sometimes I struggle to separate my own experiences from hers or what I project her feelings and experiences might be. This adoption thing is hard work all around.

As an adoptee I am constantly confronting and challenging bad adoption tropes and putting the adoptee perspective front and center. In my parenting role I am even more vigorous. I pay attention to details. Bad adoption language and misguided subtexts are not going to happen around me if I can help it. My daughter is not *lucky*. Whispers asking if she is adopted are met with strong replies that yes she is, and so am I. Claiming adoption for both of us in public feels like a way to normalize being adopted while redirecting the attention towards me (and this strategy generally stops the conversation because most people don't know what to say to an adult adopted person). My husband and I curate the adoption books we read with her and talk about those parts of a story that may not match what we know about adoption. When a story begins with a child being adopted we talk about how all children grow in their mother's tummy and that is where the story, everyone's story, truly begins. She chooses the language that she wants to use for her experiences. When she says *real* to refer to her birth family we do not correct her— they are real, they are very real to her, and we are not threatened by that truth.

So what does this all look like? Most of the time adoption it is just a matter of fact thing, a quiet background music that we hum along to. Sometimes the beat bangs a little louder. A few months ago on the drive to school (isn't it always during a drive?) she asked out of the blue, "Why did my real mother not want me?" I pulled over as quickly as I could and got into the back seat with her. I wrapped her in my arms and told her I didn't know why, I understood her hurt but I couldn't explain why that happened to her. We just hugged. I did not try to make it better for her, I didn't say that at least she had a mommy and daddy now...I just held her, listened and felt. She knows I get it because she knows I've been there, too.

One day, when my daughter was six, she asked what if she had been matched with different parents, what if I had not become her mommy? Would I still love her? Ugh. What a question. How do you explain the randomness and fragility of adoption to a six year old? You just do it. You tell the truth. Then I asked her "If you didn't know me and I wasn't your mommy would you still love *me*?" "Maybe a tiny bit," she said.

Sometimes I screw up. We were in Maui for one of my husband's conferences. Our hotel had an amazing pool area with a series of waterslides connecting half dozen tropical watering holes. My daughter and I spent an entire day holding hands while swishing and sliding between pools. It was magical. In my euphoria I blurted out "Who is your favorite mommy?" I regretted those words as soon as they came out of my mouth. What a set-up for a child— asking her to reassure me of her loyalty. How many times had my adoptive family asked the same of me? I quickly added "...uh, I mean, who is your favorite mommy today?" hoping to sort of fix the question without looking like too much of a jerk. Her response was perfection: "The mommy I knew for one day when I was born is my favorite, but you are my second favorite!" No hesitation whatsoever. This little girl is the one flipping the script now and I could not be more proud.

Weapons Of The Weak

We are walking open wounds,
no scabs to keep
the micro-aggressions out.

A time-lapse of torment and oppression,
Remnants of the war never ended.
Broken.
And fractured.
And forgotten.

Yet, the marks on our mother's skin
Prove our existence.
Her bones ache from the memory
Of a million things
I don't know how to say.

Profits increase the demand
For our separations
We are transactions,
A cause, and a commission.

But they can't sell us all.
The weapons of the weak remain strong.

We refuse to be forgotten.
Our scars are beauty marks
The wrinkles
The cracks
The quivers
They are not signs of weakness

But symbols of strengths
Yet to be discovered

We can't fly,
But we float between histories.
We can't walk through walls,
But we see the invisible.
We are terrified,
But we are not alone.

Pain is like a home-cooked meal,
Meant to be shared
In the safety of good friends

A break in my voice
Is better than only silence
And the only way to change the world
Is to let our stories breathe free.

Off Book

DURING THE SECOND HALF OF my third grade year, I was cast as Willy Wonka in the class production of "Charlie and the Chocolate Factory." I was excited, of course, but it seemed like my mother was even more excited. The day I got the part, I came home with the thick script with a green cover.

"I'm so proud of you!" my mother said. She took the script from me and flipped through it. "You have so many lines! We'll start practicing right away."

This was different. My parents didn't read, and they weren't interested in the theater— or music or art, for that matter. They liked TV and movies in a passive sort of way, but that was it. Me? I was crazy about all of them— a voracious reader, an obsessive fan of sitcoms, hour-long detective shows, and just about every movie, and enchanted by comic books and Motown songs. Even by age nine, I knew there was a distance between my parents in I, not just in what we liked, but how we approached the world.

I chalked it up to being adopted.

But to suddenly have my mother latch on to me as the equivalent to the greatest fictional candy-maker in the history of literature? It was disarming. Normally stoic and passive, my mother was suddenly animated and energetic. Whenever we went anywhere— grocery shopping, to the doctor's office, on the short drive to my grandparents' house— I had the script with me and we ran lines.

"—And the snozberries taste like snozberries!" I said.

My mother picked up the next line. "Mr. Wonka, what's a snozberry?"

"Why, a snozberry is a… It's a… I can't remember."

She handed the script back to me. "Okay, read it again and we'll try it in a few minutes."

We ran lines in the car. We ran lines at dinner. We ran lines while I played outside on the swing set in our front yard, shouting out a monologue on Oompa-Loompas while I zipped down the slide.

"Why do I have to keep doing this?" I said after about a month of practice. "I know all the lines."

"If you don't keep practicing, you'll forget them," she said. "And if you forget them, it'll be more work to learn them all again."

"Okay," I said, sullenly. "I found the Oompa-Loompas many years ago…"

In retrospect, my family— particularly my mother and her father, who I was named for— loved scripts. We had plenty of them, all unwritten but memorized through ceaseless practice and performed every day. There was the script my parents followed when my grandfather called each day after they got home from work. I only heard my parents' side, but it always went like this:

"Hello Larry. Yes, I'm home. No, I just got home. Yes, work was fine. No, nothing happened. No, I'm— that's none of your business. Yes, he's fine. I don't know. No, I don't know what we're having for dinner. How are you?"

And there was the script my parents themselves followed when it came time to decide what to have or where to go for dinner:

"What do you want for dinner? I don't care, that's fine. No, I said that's fine. Well, what do you want? Fine, we'll have that. No, it's fine. I said it's fine."

But the most common script of all was the one about my adoption. My mother especially recited it often— mostly in the years before I started school and then less so over time. "You're adopted, and that makes you special, because it means God chose you especially for us."

Early on, I remember asking, "What about my birth mother? Why did she give me up?"

And my mother would reply, "Your mother loved you so very much, but she was in college and couldn't take care of you. And so she gave you up for adoption, and God led you to us."

And by the time I was in third grade, I had this script down cold. I was off book. When I met other adults, my mother encouraged me to share my adoption story. And so I'd begin: "I'm adopted, and that makes me special because..."

We stuck to that script for years. I got older, stumbled into an awkward adolescence, retreated into books and movies. My mother started working nights at a nursing home, and whatever maternal energy she had shifted from our family to a new one— a couple dozen men and women with Alzheimer's and dementia on whom she doted. And my dad, a truck driver, grew more withdrawn, lonely, and less adept at hiding the nightly whiskey and cigarettes he swore he wasn't having.

But we played our parts. The dutiful mother. The dependable father. The devoted son. For years, my parents had hanging on the living room wall a framed copy of the letter from Catholic Charities telling them they'd been approved to adopt me. A series of portraits of me, from infancy to my latest school photo, ringed the living room walls. There were few pictures up of us as a family, just me, the reluctant star of some show.

The script kept us locked in place, always moving forward. As time went on, we spoke less and less about my adoption. I stopped asking about my birth mother because there was nothing to ask. The agency had told us everything— she was in college in northern New Hampshire, she had a sister— and the fantasies I'd had as a child about meeting her sputtered out. We didn't know other families who had adopted children. In the rare instance we'd encounter adoption— usually in one of the Sunday night made-for-TV movies my parents watched— my mother would speak up. "No matter what happens," she'd say, "I'll always be your *real* mother."

I staged minor rebellions. In high school, I stopped volunteering at the nursing home my mother worked at, ending a two-year streak of calling bingo games for the residents every Tuesday night. I bargained my way out of weekly mass, agreeing to go be confirmed at our Catholic church so long as I could stop going to services immediately after. And when I began applying to colleges, I set my sights on Dartmouth and other schools in northern New Hampshire. I thought about spending hours in some quiet campus library, looking through yearbooks for a woman with a face like mine. I thought about having my own story.

"So," my mother says. "How much longer do you have in school?"

It's the spring of 2011 and I'm finishing up my second year of graduate school. I'm 29; finally working toward the degree in writing I've wanted ever since I finished college seven years earlier. And I'm finally writing about my adoption. It's simple, exploratory stuff, essays about the night I received in the mail a copy of my original birth certificate with my birth mother's name on it, or the afternoon I found her photo in an old yearbook in a quiet campus library. About all I've learned of her and her family— *my* family— through late-night Google searches. Writing down the basic facts is hard; admitting that I have emotions— complicated emotions, in fact— about being adopted is nearly impossible. But I'm doing it, cobbling the pieces together into some sort of thesis manuscript. I think it might eventually become a book.

My mother knows this, but always seems to forget. We already have a script, so why write something else? So we keep having this conversation.

"Just another year," I say. "I'll finish this semester, and then next fall I have two more classes. After that, I have to finish my thesis in the spring. That's it."

"Oh, that's good," she says. We're at my grandparents' house. I'm there for one of my increasingly infrequent visits, and we're going through the motions of normal conversation. "What is your thesis about?"

"I'm writing about my adoption," I say. "About how I've never met my birth mother, but I know so much about her from the internet, and how other people who were adopted are in the same boat."

"Oh. So you're still writing about your adoption. That's good, I guess," she says.

"Yup."

She pauses, frowns, and looks at me. "So," she says. "How's your car running?"

A few months later, I'm at a conference on adoption in Provincetown, Mass. I'm there to do research for my thesis, to take notes, conduct interviews, and get material so I can start writing in September. But I'm overwhelmed. The speakers and panelists introduce themselves. "I'm an adoptee," they say. Or "I'm a birth father." Or "I'm an adoptive parent." Until now, all my research has been book-based. I'm beginning to understand adoption in the abstract sense, beginning to sense the dimensions of a loss I'd never allowed myself to think about.

But this is disarming. For three days, speaker after speaker shares their stories. They're honest, open. In each adoptee's story, I hear echoes of my own, sometimes faint, sometimes strong. During a session on the myths of adoption and the roles, whether conscious or unconscious, adoptees take on— the family savior, the outsider, the thankful, perpetual child— I'm so flabbergasted by these revelations I'm barely able to scribble in my notebook.

On a Friday afternoon, I have drinks with three of the speakers, a poet, a priest, and a psychiatrist. We sit on a waterfront deck sipping cocktails and shielding our eyes from the bright July sun.

"So, what's your story?" the priest asks.

I take a few sips of my gin and tonic, steady my nerves. "Well, I was adopted when I was three months old and…" The rest pours out of me. The loneliness, the loss, the longing for some kind of reply from my birth mother, whom I wrote to four years earlier and never, received a reply.

When I finish, the psychiatrist says, "It sounds like you should try again. Write another letter. Have you tried calling?"

"No," I say. "I— I just didn't think I could do that. Like I didn't have permission."

"Of course you do," she says. "Of course you do."

And now, four years later, I'm still pushing up against the script that was written for me some 30 years ago. I am still trying to fill in the details about my first mother and father and a whole family which was so neatly excised from my story. But I'm also still writing my book, still uncovering the ways, small and large, adoption has shaped me and my family. I'm writing my own lines and running them again and again, until the story becomes my own.

LYNN GRUBB

ESSAY

Adoptees Are The True Experts On Adoption

I WAS AT A MEETING AT work one day last year and we were throwing around ideas for employee morale. I suggested an employee spotlight, where a different employee each month is highlighted and can discuss their hobbies, interests, etc.

I volunteered to be the first one. I discussed with a couple members of the team bringing in a few of the adoption anthologies I had contributed to and briefly talked about my writing as an adoptee, as I had never shared this aspect of my life with my co-workers previously. One of the other employees in the meeting thought it was a great idea and commented to me,

"If you want to know more about adoption, there are a lot of adoptive parents that work at the other branch."

Without missing a beat, I replied,

"Well, thanks, but I have been adopted every day for 48 years."

My co-worker meant well— she was just reacting like most people would— seeing adoptive parents as the "experts" in adoption. I find it curious that adoptive parents— the ones who many times are muddling through an experience that they were ill-prepared to handle— are most often seen as experts.

I asked myself on many occasions before #flipthescript (the social media movement), "Why adoptee voices are missing from national media outlets like National Public Radio, world and local news and, mainstream movies and books (except for orphan/savior themes)? Why are our voices left out of the chorus?"

Traditionally, adoptees have been subtly silenced without even realizing it. Adoptees, as a group, like to blend in with others and the last thing we really want is to draw attention to the differences that we already felt growing up. It's a rare adopted person who wants to be an "adoptee spokesperson".

This "blending in" of adoptees so as not to appear different contributes to our voices being unheard; however that is not the full story. For some reason, it is just easier for many to believe that if adoption is involved, everything worked out in the end. We all lived happily ever after. We see promotions on television for pet adoption, but you rarely see pets post-adoption being shown at six months or six years in the future in their new homes. It is just assumed that "an adopted pet is a happy pet." I'm sorry to say, we assume the same thing about adoptees.

This assumption that adoptees will have no issues or problems post-adoption was brought home to me when I tried a handful of different therapists throughout my 30s and 40s, none of whom had any training regarding adoption.

That is why #flipthescript campaign was so important in order to educate those who are in the helping profession, adoptive families, and the general public and even pastors who incorrectly preach that legal adoption is the same as adoption by God. Education is sorely needed by so many.

The #flipthescript campaign gave voice to what was formerly only shared between like-minded adoptees. We are a growing chorus using our creative outlets and experience, along with social media, to say:

Adoptees are the experts on adoption. Listen to us.

How different would that conversation at work have been if my coworker had said,

> *"Wow, Lynn, with you being adopted, I bet you have some interesting viewpoints that the rest of us would love to hear."*

Usually when I discuss my adoptee writing, activism and my experiences growing up in a closed adoption, many times, I am asked about my "real parents" and how they feel— mind you, I'm never really sure which "real parents" people are inquiring about as that changes depending on the inquirer.

Those of us who speak out and say things that are difficult for others inside and outside of the adoption community to hear, are breaking the status quo and receiving push-back to the idea that adoptee voices should be seen as the experts. Understandably, people are resistant to change.

Those of us who flip the script are conquering adoption myths of "birth parent confidentiality", discrimination as to how adoptees' birth documents are treated (this includes step-parent adoptions and even in-family adoptions), and publicly writing in order to conquer the many stereotypes that are rampant about adoptees and adoption. Many of us, myself included, are no longer comfortable with being invisible in adoption policy and law.

This is one of the reasons I began writing about adoption. My voice was being drowned out by how everybody else viewed adoption and what they thought. I didn't like what I saw being portrayed in the media about adoption.

Just turn on the television during National Adoption Month, and the only voices you hear are the "experts" in adoption (adoptive parents, therapists, attorneys), which I could bet dollars to donuts, rarely are any of them adopted. Even though these "experts" in the media are rarely giving voice to the adoptee experience— those voices have become the accepted "party line" in society making it difficult for true adoptee voices to become mainstream. We need a more realistic view of adoption and adoptees can provide that much-needed balance.

My writing about adoption in a public forum is about taking back my personal power as an adopted person and empowering other adoptees to do the same. One of my most popular blogs is titled, "Please Stop Glamorizing Adoption!" In that blog I discuss how I can't turn on my TV without adoption being used, promoted or glamorized in movies or reality TV in a very superficial way. Black and white thinking about adoption does everyone a disservice. I would really like to see a TV show about adoption free of stereotypes and clichés and heavy on the emotional complexities that adoptees actually live with.

It was very scary and intimidating when I first began writing about adoption. I feared what other people would say and think, but what I feared even more is that the general public would never hear or understand my experiences as an adoptee, had I not contributed to the conversation. This breaking out of the "adoptee closet" and writing publicly is how I own the title of "Adoptee". I may not have chosen to be adopted, but I get to choose what I do with that title.

I was at a child abuse training session a few years back and a speaker came to talk about adoption. I noticed that the legalities and the process of adoption was something that was covered, but there was no mention of how adoptees experience their own adoptions. I find this ludicrous! It seems that once the ink is dry on the paperwork, nobody feels the need to find out the rest of the story from the actual people that grow up living the experience. I asked the speaker privately what one had to do to become an expert in adoption. She replied, "Get a Master's Degree".

I found that kind of funny. Here she was talking to a person who was adopted every day of her life, but this woman, who was not adopted, became an "expert" by obtaining a master's degree. (I admit degrees help, but they cannot replace living the actual experience).

Adoptees have lived adoption. We have experienced it. You may not hear all positive, happy thoughts, but we have something valuable to share when we write, speak, act, film or paint. Listen to our joys, our heartaches, our opinions, our feelings. Listen to our stories about what our parents did right, and what they could have done better, had they been properly educated. Listen to our stories of abuse so as to prevent future abuses. Listen to our positive experiences so those experiences can be the norm. Listen to our opinions about adoption policy and law, and treat us as equal to all other citizens when handling our original identities.

Become educated about adoption by going to the horse's mouth and reading adoptee-authored anthologies, memoirs and blogs like Lost Daughters. Go to adoption conferences that feature adopted adults who speak about their experiences. Attend an adoption support group and listen to adoptees speak. Fight beside adoptees that still cannot access their original birth certificates in a majority of states in the U.S. by writing your representatives in support of equal access.

You can also support documentary film makers, such as Jean Strauss, Ann Fessler, and Bryan Tucker, who more accurately portray the adoptee experience in media.

Adoptees are the true experts on adoption.

It's time to listen to us.

Flip the Script.

Strenghth Of The Broken

WRITER'S NOTE: WHEN I FINALLY came up with a title for my memoir I was inspired to write a song with the title but one that also expressed that I know that there are many "like me" who feel these or very similar emotions. And this is my dedication lyrically to all of you that have felt broken but remain strong through adversity, foster care and adoption. My hope for this song is that it will give hope that strength can be found on days where one may feel lost, confused, scared, unwanted and broken. -Liz

When you don't know your real name
When you feel lost and sometimes afraid
You have the strength of the broken
Strength of the broken
Strength of the broken
Strength of the broken
I know the pain will never leave
And there's many others like you and me
We have the strength of the broken
Strength of the broken
Strength of the broken
Strength of the broken
I know the pain will never leave
I know sometimes life don't seem fair
I know somedays it feels like nobody cares
You have strength of the broken
Strength of the broken
Strength of the broken
Strength of the broken
When you just want a real home
But you find yourself standing out here all alone
You have the strength of the broken
Strength of the broken

Strength of the broken
Strength of the broken
Reapeat
When you don't know your real name
When you feel lost and sometimes afraid
You have the strength of the broken
Strength of the broken
Strength of the broken
Strength of the broken
Strength of the broken

Hometown

WRITER'S NOTE: HOMETOWN IS A song which I was inspired to write for the adoption community. It was written to hopefully be a tool to help us get something that we are denied. "Our identity" I wanted to help the lawmakers understand the huge and unfair impact it has on a person, of going through life not knowing ones identity. In the lyrics I suggest that the lawmakers try to imagine if it was them that did not know who they were. It is not something that most people can imagine however, there are millions of people and this is there reality. I want to use my gift to help people understand that this must change as it is inhumane. This song is intended to help adoptees receive their original birth certificates. Yes, I have a dream!

I've been wandering too long
Trying to belong
I've been wandering too long
Trying to be strong
Where's my hometown?
Cause, I don't know, don't know
Where's my hometown?"
Cause I don't know, don't know
See we don't know
We don't know
We don't know
We don't know
Don't know Don't know Don't know
Who am I?
Can you tell me?
Who am I?

Who am I?
Can you tell me?
Who am I?
Now you might not understand
But you have the upper hand
So what if it was you?
Wandering too...
Asking...
Where's my hometown?
Cause you didn't know, didn't know
Where's my hometown?
Cause you didn't know didn't know
Just wandering... wondering
Wandering...wondering
Who am I?
Can you tell me?
Who am I?
Who am I?
I don't know, don't know, don't

CHRISTINE SATORY

ART

CHOSEN (2015)
Mixed-media: drawing and personal photographs.

THE FRAUD (2015)

Mixed-media: drawing and personal photographs.

A LOVING GIFT (2015)

Mixed-media: drawing and personal photographs.

KAYE PEARSE

ESSAY

Chosen

————◆————

"**C**HOSEN." IT IS ONE OF those words that raise ire among many adult adoptees. It elicits the image of a large store where prospective parents peruse row after row of cribs in search of the perfect infant: Blondes with curls— Aisle 1, Brunettes with dimples— Aisle 3. The reality is that very few adoptees— especially the ones placed at birth— were actually chosen by their parents. More likely is that an expectant mother selected an agency, and when her child was born, the couple at the top of the agency's waiting list received a call: "We have a healthy, white …" "Yes! We'll take it!"

And still, adoptive parents tell their children that they have been "chosen." Perhaps it's an attempt to make the child less insecure about having been given up to begin with. Perhaps it's a religious belief ("You were chosen by God to be our child"). Regardless the reason, it's almost always untrue, yet something many adoptees have heard at some point in their lives. Much has been written elsewhere on this topic, and I won't rehash that topic here.

It wasn't until I was in my 50's that I discovered a vast online community of adult adoptees, each with a different story to tell, and it was in that community that I first learned of the distaste towards the idea of being "chosen." When I mentioned the word in an introductory post detailing my adoption story, a group of adoptees immediately jumped into the thread to inform me of the word's hollowness, its untruthfulness, its hurtfulness. I was embarrassed and contrite. I tried to explain my choice of words, and that I hadn't meant to offend; but the respondents were unforgiving, letting me know that the damage had been done. With that revelation, I vowed I'd never use the word again, even when discussing my own life.

My adoption history can best be described as atypical. Taken from my mother at the age of 16 months, I was adopted by relatives. They hadn't planned to adopt a child; there was no burning desire to parent a toddler, but when circumstances made adoption appear necessary, they took me in and did their best. They told me I was adopted because my mother "couldn't take care of me". There was no carefully-crafted adoption book, no story of how they'd been wishing and praying for a child and how happy they were to have me. My adoption was simply a matter of fact, unavoidable, event. Unfortunately, upon the death of his wife a few years later, my aging adoptive father was left feeling overwhelmed by the prospect of being the single parent of a barely-manageable pre-teen girl. He arranged for my adoption to be dissolved so that I could be re-adopted by a different family member.

Again, I was told that I was being given up because a parent "couldn't take care of me". The second adoption was as equally matter of fact as the first.

However, there was one important difference. The reality was that these relatives didn't want to adopt me, and only agreed to do so out of a misplaced sense of obligation. I was a family responsibility, a burden, an unwelcome presence in their home. I was told I was ill-behaved, that I was rude, and that I was ungrateful and spoiled. No longer an only child, I was expected to assume my new status of middle sibling with ease and complacency. The family member who'd been my adoptive father quickly released himself from that role and no longer treated me differently from any other child in the family. Once I had been his daughter, now I was no longer special to him in any obvious way.

My new parents didn't hide their displeasure with the situation. Instead of treating me with kindness, they treated me with disdain. Instead complimenting me for my accomplishments, they berated me for not doing better. Instead of appreciating me for my talents, they told me I was inadequate. Instead of acknowledging the difficulties leading to my relinquishment, they brusquely informed me that my birth mother simply didn't want me. Instead of affection, they dispensed abuse.

Instead of reassurances that I was loved and valued, there was silence.

It was in this emotional void that I spent the bulk of my childhood. To fill the emptiness, I created a vivid world of make-believe in which I imagined that I was cared about by a multitude of friends and family. In my diary, I chronicled my adolescent hopes that someday the fantasy would become reality. Nightly, I made the same wish on the first visible star: "I wish I could be happy in everything I do." I also dreamt regularly of escape; of running in terror from those who would imprison and hurt me. On the frequent occasions when I was unable to summon any optimism about the future, I contemplated suicide.

Ultimately, my childhood hopes never came to fruition and, though I survived, I was unable to fully overcome the numerous struggles I faced. For me, the lesson of multiple abandonments was that permanency is an illusion, and that when a situation becomes difficult, the best way to handle it is to walk away. I discovered that dearly wanting something results in its eventual denial. I learned early that I was unlovable, and that to trust others guarantees only sorrow.

Since that time I was criticized so harshly online, I've come to realize that all adoption histories have value, and that all voices deserve to be heard. Because of that, I am flipping the script on my own fellow adoptees and, while I sincerely empathize with those for whom something represents emptiness and falsehood, I will no longer deny my own truth.

As a child, there were so many things I longed to believe— that I was special, that I was wanted, that I was loved. This one word that so many others despise is something I desperately needed to hear, and its absence helped to leave my soul battered and scarred. Condemn me if you will, that is your right, but know that my heart truly aches for the one simply fantasy it was always denied:

I was chosen.

MI OK SONG BRUINING

POETRY

We Don't All Look Alike

We don't all look alike—
some of us are short,
a few are taller and lanky
with finer bones and chiseled features.

some of us pull our hair back with barrettes.
A few of us have longer "black" hair
cascading down our strong backs.

some of us wear dyke-like
spike haircuts to offset our
gentle, but never quiet spirits
of our ancestors' blood
that washed laundry and built
the railroads to gold mountain.

some of us have mixed blood
with larger than almond-shaped eyes,
lighter hair and freckles, but
we hail and prevail from the same
ancestral soil of the fields,
villages and cities
we or our parents were
born into with pride and cultures,
cultivated for thousands of undocumented years.

some of us, and our mothers and grandmothers
arrived as paper daughters—
immigrants at the airports, angel island,
internment camps, refugee boats,

pieces of us dying or killing
a part of our identities with name changes
and whitened lies into "truths."

some of us have lived in thailand,
indonesia, malaysia, bangladesh,
on the islands of the philippines and hawaii,
in past lives or visiting
in our dreams.

some of us have accents when we speak,
are bi-lingual, tri-lingual,
speaking tagolog, hangul, cantonese,
mandarin, or toisanese,
or are english-speaking only
our tongues spitting out
the stereotypes that have shackled
and chained us together.

some of us are deaf
and hard of hearing
listening with our eyes
and talking with our hands.

some of us are differently-abled,
sitting ten feet tall in wheelchairs,
spinning around in grace on the dance floor
with our friends, back and forth.

some of us are adopted, with whitened
childhoods and buried pasts
shrouded in mystery and the lost
secrets of our invisible birth mothers.

some of us live and work
in chinatowns, japantowns, koreatowns,
little thailands, little indias,
little vietnams—our own villages,
neighborhoods and communities
who welcome us
as pilippinas, pacific islanders, south asians,

canadians, hapas, issei, nissei—
with the smell of kimchi and baos,
the clatter of chopsticks over dim sum
and check out the "bad asian dykes"
over at the next table!

some of us are educated, over-educated,
academic, intellectual, creative,
working class, garment workers,
professionals, students, artists,
and construction workers—tough,
muscle-bound dykes
who strut and swagger with unbound feet
and never are we docile,
obedient, soft-spoken, and exotic
playthings to be tokenized.
We are all sisters, but

We don't all look alike.

Not Just Another One Of Those Identity Poems

Who Am I?

I am a Woman
whose Korean given name translates into
"Beautiful Jade"—
a polished, translucent stone.
I was born in Tae Han Min Guk—
the Land of the Morning Calm,
somewhere
south of Pon Mun Jom,
in my native tongue—
the 38th Parallel, to you.
I became the human version
of an imported product
stamped "Made in Korea."

Who Am I?

I am adopted—a Paper Daughter,
exported at the age of five
under "Alien" immigration status
to the u.s., as the 1,000th
adopted Korean child, during the first
of four waves
of the international adoption industry
to a suburban, upper middle class
Wonder bread white family.

I was given a new anglo first name
and given all the white-washed,
privileged trappings
and social conditioning,
which choked and gagged me
into silence
for twenty years.

Who Am I?

I am a Woman, a Woman of Colour—born
in the Year of the Rat,
but I celebrate a fictitious birthday,
whose date is unknown,
with a birth name and a family name
whose origins are unknown—
scrawled on incomplete, faded,
undocumented records.
But, they are all
I have to call my own.

Who Am I?

I am a Sister—strong,
angry and powerful
who struggles
in the heterosexist, misogynist
and homophobic trenches
against queer-bashing,
stereotyping,
the "Asian Model Minority" myth,
the plexi-glass ceiling,
the mail order bride industry,
baby trafficking,
exotica erotica,
sexploitation and fear.

Who Am I?

I am an artist and wanna-be writer
who believes writing is a political act

where words are power
and knowledge is power
and words and knowledge can be used
as weapons for social change
and political justice.

Who Am I?

I am the youngest
of four children in a family
who will never know
my secrets, my pride, my strength,
my pain, my struggles,
and my power.
Sticks and stones haven't broken
my bones,
but names have always hurt me.

Who Am I?

I am the small child you see
with the haunting look
in my eyes of longing and aching
to belong to myself.

I am also the adopted
Korean Womanist,
who is doing it for myself
through working, writing,
fighting and speaking
through process, changes,
growth and celebration.

JOSHUA CROME
Essay

#FlipTheScript, the social media movement, was a great experience for me. I was able to express what I thought about adoption, and the movement introduced me to a community of people who are seeking to get the voices and concerns of adoptees heard. It's vital that our concerns be acknowledged and acted on. We need to be active in pressing for repeal of closed records laws and reform of adoption. Adoption is portrayed, in our popular culture and the media, as The Greatest Thing Ever. It's a lot more complex than it's portrayed by "Diff'rent Strokes" and "Webster", and the people who deal with the complexities most acutely are the adoptees. Through #FlipTheScript, I've received help with my search for family, and I've been fortunate enough to help others find people who can help them with their searches.

Growing up in a family where three of my four siblings were also adoptees made adoption seem more normal. I knew we stuck out like sore thumbs to others, but within our crew we were normal. I think that sense of normalcy played a big role in my relatively positive attitude about adoption as a kid and a young adult.

What caused me to look for my natural/birth/original family? (I still wrestle with the added terminology that search and reunion has added to my vocabulary.) A few things come to mind:

- Raising a family, and seeing my kids' similarities to me caused me to start thinking about just who do I take after?

- Being a history nerd and realizing that I knew almost nothing about my own history.

- Wondering if my sister had access to her family's medical history, could it have saved her life?

- Being told I have no place in my adoptive family.

Getting cast out by my adoptive family was extremely painful. I wondered- and still do- would they have done the same to their own blood? What is it actually like being a blood relation? Pain turned to anger, and anger gave way to what I've heard described as a quiet resolve: I was going to search for my biological family. Being on the outs with my a-parents gave me the freedom to not have to care what they might have thought about me looking for my birth family. I started looking around for how to search. I signed up for the Illinois Adoption Registry and its Medical Information Exchange. Through that process, I learned that Illinois had passed a law that would allow Illinois adoptees to obtain a non-certified copy of their original birth certificate. I sent my application to Springfield by overnight delivery, and waited through six months of backlog- over 8,000 adoptees deep. Finally, it arrived and I couldn't wait to open it. What I saw was life-altering.

I had a <u>name</u>. My mother cared enough for me to name me. This is profound. When I was kicked out of my adoptive family, my brother (my a-parents' biological son) told me to "Change your name. It is not yours". Knowing that I've always had a name has helped to lessen the pain of being cast out from the family I grew up in. I had my mother's name, place and of birth, address at the time I was born. I had enough information to look, and it was MY information, my simple piece of paper.

Two years after receiving my OBC, I'm playing with the house's money. I've been able to find and reunite with my mom, dad, siblings, aunts, uncles, and grandparents. I'm still humbled by the uniformity of the welcome by everyone and am excited about the positive impact reunion is having, and will have, on my family and me. People from time to time say to me that I'm courageous for putting myself out there and looking. I'd respond to that by pointing out that a whole bunch of people also had the courage to be found and to reach out to me.

I don't think I'm necessarily anti-adoption. There are so many wonderful adoptive parents, birth parents, and adoptees who I know, and I can look back to my own experience to know that there are indeed positive aspects to adoption. I am, however, very critical of adoption in a way I wasn't years ago. I believe sealed records are wrong. I've seen firsthand what happens to adoptees when the lack of family medical and health history becomes an issue in diagnosing an illness. I believe that adoption being a $13 billion industry is wrong, and that the adoption industry in the United States differs from outright human trafficking only by degree. I believe that the industry does not do sufficient due diligence on prospective APs because they are the paying clients. Agencies do not care about adoptees and birth parents once the deal is made and the money has changed hands. The institution of adoption is crying out for reform, and adoptees need to play a leading role in the reform effort.

AMIRA ROSE DAVIS

POETRY

Unmasked

A POEM OF ADOPTION AND REUNION

OF SCARS AND OF HEALING

(INCLUDES TEXT FROM *WE WEAR THE MASK* POEM BY PAUL LAURENCE DUNBAR)

We wear the mask that grins and lies,
It hides our cheeks and shades our eyes,—
This debt we pay to human guile;
With torn and bleeding hearts we smile,
And mouth with myriad subtleties.

I was born…
with flowers in bloom, as spring gave way to summer.
Born under the shade of forgotten slave trees,
their bark still wet from the juice of strange fruit.
Born inhaling the sweet Texas hear-the air heavy with possibility

I was born.

Feeling.

But I did not *see* her. I did not *hear* her.

That rhythmic melody that I had danced to for 9 months?
Suddenly gone.
Her voice? Mute.
Her face-that I had been so eager to touch? Far from my tiny reach.

painful silence cut fast and sharp
wounding me deep beneath the surface of my brown baby skin

and Yet,

I did not cry.

Everyone says I was a happy baby- the foster family, the social worker, my new
parent-what a *happy happy* baby, always giggling, always smiling...

I had already perfected my mask,
and I wore it proudly

Why should the world be over-wise,
In counting all our tears and sighs?
Nay, let them only see us, while
We wear the mask.

And I grew...
in the foothills of New England
Grew among the mountains,
and autumn leaves,
nestled deep in "happy valley".

I grew
little black girl
lesbian moms
German last name,
and a near perfect smile

Grew
as I tip toped over landmines,
Mothers day, my birthday, family tree projects, biology class...
I walked with the grace of a drunk giraffe,
bumping head first into an emotional bomb
Ready to explode
to rip of my mask and expose my wounds...

But I kept smiling.

I spun fairy tales like a web,
Weaving dreams of my parents into emotional safety net.
She was famous
I'd say

He was an athlete
I'd say
It just wouldn't be fair to have a baby on the road...

Little black orphan Annie, wailing *Maybe* out the window
My open wounds glistening in the moon light...

We smile, but, O great Christ, our cries
To thee from tortured souls arise.
We sing, but oh the clay is vile
Beneath our feet, and long the mile;
But let the world dream otherwise,
We wear the mask!

Loneliness is a bitch.
And I was hurting,
Silently, alone
And I couldn't stop the bleeding
Couldn't even find the wound...

But my moms were there.
I nestled between them as they created a fortress around me
and together we found the cut...

A deep gash-
from many years ago.

They help me take off my mask and together we embraced the pain
I don't have to smile
Grateful and Happy aren't the only things I have to feel
I don't have to shit rainbows and frolic with butterflies just because I am adopted

I. DON'T. HAVE. TO. SMILE.

And now- it doesn't hurt as bad,
a scar that I can see and feel and touch
its engraved on me
but not bleeding anymore...
it still hurts
but it's not bleeding anymore.

Until …
SHE comes back
or rather
I stumble upon her
and suddenly she's back,
the melody of her heart
her face
her scent smashing into me like a two ton brick
my flesh ripping open
my wounds dripping

Instinctively I smile..,
I reach for my mask, that slides on so easy
and I smile…

I smile
amid the "you're so lucky"
I smile
at the "that is so heartwarming"
I smile
As people applaud the end of a story that is not yet finished.

Smile…"you look just like her"
Smile…"she's still married to your dad!"
Smile…"you have siblings!"
Smile…"they are excited to meet you"
Smile…"now you have one big family!"
Smile…"a *real* family"
Smile…aren't you so happy??

Smile
Smile
Smile
Smile

Smile so hard
my mask breaks
shattering under the weight of complex feelings.
I am standing there-
drenched from the tidal wave of emotion

ADULT ADOPTEE ANTHOLOGY

anger
and pain
and joy
and guilt
and love
and hate
and relief

I can feel them all.
I am ALLOWED to feel them all.

Adoptees aren't robots programmed to one "happy" setting
We are people with a full range of emotions.
Don't try to program me.
Don't try to box me in.
Don't try to make me a adoption poster child.
In fact don't make me a child at all.
I am a grown ass women...

I am an *adult* adoptee
I am black with white parents- but also with black parents,
I am straight with gay parents- but also with straight parents
I am the product of 4 family lines
I have 3 moms and a dad.
I am a mom, I am a wife, I am a sister, I am a daughter, I
am a student I am a teacher I am a friend...

I am a know it all who knows that she doesn't know it all
A social butterfly whose lonely in a room full of people
I am fiercely independent but I crave constant connection
I am wrapped in Texas sun and kissed by New England snow
I am the embodiment of contradictions
but don't you dare try to diminish the fullness of my identity.

I will no longer shrink my existence to fit behind a painted on smile...

Adoption
Reunion
can hurt
can heal
can hurt some more.

140

I proudly wear my scars
They are tattooed on the very fabric of my being…

I stand here,
scarred and smiling

I am me-
fully
completely
and unmasked

ZARA PHILLIPS
Essay & Lyrics

The Road To Freedom

A S A SMALL CHILD I would spend hours in my bedroom playing all my Mother's Broadway records. She often played them when she was cooking, filling the house with music. I would meticulously write down all the lyrics, playing each line, lifting the needle, until I had all the words. Once finished, I would place my dolls and teddy bears in rows across my bed and my floor and would "perform" to my favorite songs in a heartfelt passionate way. I was told, however, that my voice was too deep to be chosen for parts in the school plays.

I did not consider myself talented, nor did I sing for that reason. All I knew at the time was that singing made me feels less alone. I felt transported, lifted up. Singing gave me a channel, a place outside of myself where I could relegate all the hurt, a place that was mystical from the very beginning.

I moved from singing to writing. I would sit in my room quietly penning story after story. Tales of children overcoming great obstacles and when I read them out loud, adults would respond with similar comments, expressing surprise that a very young girl would write such sad stories.

I could read and write by four years old and enjoyed Kindergarten. I wrote my first poem about a river, which was exhibited in the hallway of my school for all to see. It was the first recognition of my writing ability. But I never thought about what that meant, to be recognized. I wrote story after story in my bedroom much to the surprise of my friends, because I needed to. I needed the escape to somehow make sense of what had happened to me as an adopted child and how to cope with living in such a dysfunctional home, full of silence.

I stopped writing stories when I started taking drugs, which became a way to replace the void; I stopped escaping through the written word. My world became a whirlwind of running and fixing myself.

My creativity was focused on how to get my drugs, how to manipulate people to give me what I craved in order to survive.

Soon thereafter I joined a band because a boy invited me to become a member. Becoming part of the band reawakened that familiar feeling of when I was young and had performed alone in my room. I loved to perform. I liked people watching me; it made me feel that I existed. And I began to write again but this time lyrics. I loved the challenge of writing words to a melody. Melodies that would come to me in my dreams at night— sometimes waking me so I could record them before losing them.

Within a very short time of starting to sing I was hired as a backing vocalist with well-known bands in England. In a matter of a week my life changed. I was on television, I was touring the world. Drugs and alcohol surrounded me and I consumed more of both and also sought escape with various men. My

142

work was going well; I had the most incredible experiences for someone so young. But my addictions escalated. I was still running, though in a more prestigious environment. And my soul was slowly dying.

My adopted brother had been a heroin addict for several years and I became a victim of his violence and verbal abuse. I knew he could not help himself, so I withheld the truth to protect him when people became aware that he was hurting me.

I had become a professional liar because I lived in constant fear. Fear that my adopted parents would find out about my brother's problem and fear that he would kill me.

I was surrounded by famous people, beautiful women, handsome men, who in my view, all seemed to know what they were doing. I felt like a fraud. I had no self-esteem and I lived with a sense of constant panic, only alleviated by alcohol or drugs, which boosted my confidence.

It was only when I was on stage and singing that I felt connected to something real, but I was unable to explain that to anyone.

When I was twenty-two I experienced a true awakening. A person who had been helping me looked me in the eye one early evening and said, "Zara you are twenty- two years of age. I don't know if you are going to make it to twenty-three. You have to stop running."

I have never forgotten that moment, that feeling in my solar plexus as if I had been kicked in the stomach, for I knew without a shadow of a doubt that he was right. I had been hiding my drug use from all my friends, my inability to be alone and not high. My fear when my drugs were running out, my obsession with how I was going to get more. The hole inside, a sadness that was now gaping, it was so deep within me. I felt that if I told anyone the truth I would never stop crying.

My self-hatred led me to self-harm. I put myself in relationships that were dangerous and not loving.

And my belief underneath it all that my Mother had given me away because obviously I must have done something wrong, that my conception was a big mistake, I was not meant to be here, I had to earn my right.

I went home that night after my friend had faced me with the stark truth. I got on my knees and I prayed for the first time, and I asked whoever was up there for I had no clear vision in my mind, to help me, so that I could not stop running, so that I could live. I was tired of hating myself.

I fell asleep on the floor and I remember the moon shining so brightly onto me through the curtain less windows. I felt warmth, as if being held.

The next day my desire to stay sober was overwhelming. I reached out to people in a 12-step program and I told them I was ready to fight my demons. The members of the group were gentle and ever so kind.

"One hour at a time," they told me softly. "Sometimes one minute at a time and then a day will come and then another. You can do this; you need never use a drug or drink again."

I listened and I reached out and told the famous bands that I could not work for them right then because I knew that my sobriety depended on me being in a safe environment. It was so hard because music meant everything to me. Some days I yelled at my newfound friends.

"Don't you know who I am? Don't you know what I do?'

They smiled gently and said, "Zara, we don't care who you worked for, we want you to stay sober, we want you to heal your grief. Music will come again. We want you to live."

And so I put a band together, a bunch of early twenty-year-olds, all newly sober. It was crazy: we chain smoked, and we rehearsed and played gigs and wrote songs, one after another. I felt so happy and I didn't care that the gigs we played were small into comparison to my previous concerts.

I became a lead singer; a songwriter and I loved it. I found when I was having a difficult day I no longer needed to pick up a drug or a drink; I picked up a guitar.

One of my most profound gigs was at a sober New Year's party where I was invited on stage by one of the most established musicians I had ever met.

As I strutted on the stage I looked down at the front row. It was full of all my friends, a special group, supporting one another, getting sober.

They were cheering, clapping, yelling, whistling and I felt so much love and support it stopped me in my tracks. That night I sang with passion and gratitude, thrilled to be invited onto that stage.

I found my birth mother when I was twenty-four years of age and when my emotions felt too overwhelming, I wrote songs about them.

I moved to the States and became active in the adoption community. I began to talk about my feelings.

I got married and became a Mother and I wrote more songs about my babies and then a book, *Mother Me* about my experience of finding my Mother and becoming one.

All the time getting support for my adoption feelings, going to 12 step meetings and staying sober.

I met Darryl McDaniels from DMC and we wrote a song 'I'm legit' to educate the general public about the plight of the adopted person. Darryl said to me,

"Music is the answer; it connects people; if we write a song... people will listen."

A couple of years ago I wrote a one-woman show *Beneath My father's Sky* to help deal with my grief of not knowing who my birth father is.

I was surprised at how quickly I wrote this piece but it was all there inside of me, and it has been incredibly healing on a personal level and well received by audiences, which is an added bonus.

Over a year ago I got divorced. I feared that this time I would be unable to stay sober while going through such deep pain, but I picked up the guitar and wrote a song about it.

And now I am completing my first novel about all the experiences I have gone through.

There is no doubt in my mind that the written, sung and acted word has saved me from myself over and over again. Through grieving and healing, I found my voice and by sharing my voice and my vulnerability I have connected with a community of people whom I would never have met.

I have heard so many stories of addiction, loss and pain but what I have been shown on this journey, is that love really does prevail, that by reaching out, taking the risk to ask for help changes one's whole life in ways that I had never truly imagine possible.

I was a very lost, broken hearted, depressed young woman who could not go a day without taking something to change the way I felt. I did not care if I was dead or alive and yet I had that moment of clarity because one kind person told me that I could get well. In that brief moment I believed them; I reached out my hand and others took it.

I believe that none of us can tread this road alone but together we can achieve the unimaginable.

Today my heart today is over flowing with gratitude and more peace than I have ever known. And the reason I know, is because I allowed others to see my grief, expressed it in a safe place and I have been able to move forward.

And yes, I write about this too.

I'm Legit

BY ZARA PHILLIPS
AND DARRYL McDANIELS

SOME NIGHTS I'M TOSSING AND TURNING IN MY BED,
IMAGINING YOUR FACE, BUT I KNOW WHAT IM UP AGAINST
FEELS LIKE I'M CLIMBING A MOUNTAIN, SWIMMING UPSTREAM,
HOLD ME I'M FALLING, I'M FALLING FURTHER AWAY

TELL ME DO YOU REMEMBER, WHEN YOU'RE ON THE STREETS,
DO YOU LOOK FOR ME THE WAY I LOOK FOR YOU,
HOW I WISH THAT I KNEW. I WISH I KNEW.

They say that life is a mystery and I just want to know my history what's my purpose and destiny why these secrets are kept from me I'm living my life on chapter 2 want to start on page one like you all do, are you looking for me like the way I'm looking for you this chapter of my life is called 'I wish I knew.'

MORNING COMES CAN YOU HEAR ME CALL FOR YOU,
IN THE HOPE THAT YOU WILL SOMEHOW HEAR ME TOO,
I'M UNDER THE MOONLIGHT, WHAT'S CLEAR IN THIS DARK NIGHT,
I NEED TO KNOW YOU AND TELL YOU THAT I'M OKAY

TELL ME DO YOU REMEMBER, WHEN YOU'RE ON THE STREETS,
DO YOU LOOK FOR ME THE WAY I LOOK FOR YOU,
HOW I WISH THAT I KNEW. I WISH I KNEW.
DO YOU WISH TOO?

At night I can't sleep I toss and turn my true reality is what I want to learn but they are telling me I can't see the proof on a little piece of paper that holds the truth of who I am and what I be, I'm living but I am missing a part of me I have a right to know where I come from cos it's my human right just like everyone, I'm not ashamed that I was born and how I came into this world it is not wrong my identity must identify with every part of me until I die in my own country I am living a lie cos there ashamed of me and I don't know why it's the lies that cause all the guilt and shame but the truth will set us free and kill all the pain, I'm legit, I'm legit not illegitimate and I will not quit this rhyme I will spit until I get my original birth certificate so give it up.

CHRISTOPHER WILSON

ESSAY

I Know Who I Am.

I HAVE NOT FOLLOWED CLOSELY THE flip the script social media campaign. I have seen it here and there through the window of my Facebook account but suffice to say I am not too sure of what it all entails, I assume something unique to each and every individual even if it has an underlying meaning, and I am sure it has something to do with expression. I think it's great for everyone to share their voices and viewpoints and opinions. I was asked to share mine by a dear friend and so I am, but I will warn you…I don't know much but this is what I do know…I met God. I found him, but more accurately, he found me. When he found me, he asked, "Do I know who I am?" I started to ramble about the things I was doing in my life, career wise. He interrupted and said, "No, no. You are telling me what you do. Do you know who you are?" I started talking more about things I did in my life, but he just kept interrupting me. "No, no. I am asking you, do you know who you are?" Clearly I was not getting the question. Who am I? So, a little agitated, I simply said, "I don't know, what you want me to say?" Eventually he replied, "What are you searching for?" In that moment, words came out of me that I was not quite sure where they were coming from. I hadn't really ever been searching for anything in my life to my knowledge. I was pretty content, but for some reason, I opened my mouth and said, "I am looking for my father. I have never known my father." So God sent me out on a journey. Looking for what was right in front of me.

Him, my father. My Heavenly father. I began to seek God. In everything.

And I found him.

In everything.

Including inside myself.

I realized who I was. I was his son. See, I was filled up, that hole and longing was made whole, because I filled up with God. At first I thought I was searching for my biological father when I blurted out that I am looking for my father, but God showed me that wasn't the case. He said, "Go deeper. Towards what you are truly searching. Love in an unconditional form, a purpose, and all things considered". I would never find this in any human individual or even in any task or job. Who I am as far as race or ethnicity is a deep layer of what I am, but it is not the deepest.

See, I am a child of God. His son. He is in me, I am he, and he is me. So, as I searched for God, my Heavenly father, he led me on a journey that made my entire life full.

The questions that many individuals who were adopted have— like what is my ethnic background, or what is my biological families medical history, God said, "Give those worries to me. I got you.

If you need to know something about yourself, I'll show you in my perfect timing. Just follow me. Forget all of that stuff and follow me. You aren't defined by a paper, or by anything else. I will show you everything you need to know". As I sought him, he led me to find my biological father, my birth mother, and me. But the healing in me was made through him, not them. One of the biggest blessings to me being adopted, is I am unchained. I do have a family, but the family that raised me, and the family that came together to give birth to me are part of a larger family that I am in touch with, the human race, and we are all God's creation. My brothers and sisters are those in the body of Christ with me, the ones that hear his voice. I see that. All of us are connected. I am blessed he shows me this thread of connection. I see myself in every single person, just as much as I see our Lord. Again— I say we are all connected. I could never put the pressure of my being content on a human being, parent, friend, or lover. No, why would I when a very capable God is able, willing, and pleading to do that for me. So I give it to him. Had I just found my birth parents, or my birth certificate, I would have never been whole. Because as God told me, that wasn't what I was really looking for. A part of me may have thought that, but he said, "Go deeper". So I did, and it is nothing against my birth parents. I found them. I am overjoyed. I would have the same joy had I not found them, because the joy I feel comes from God and knowing that I have given my life over to him, and I trust him, and that joy is constant, even through the pain and long-suffering we do for God (if that is who we choose to do it for) and by doing it for him, the pain is no longer in vain. There is joy in that, yes! So the joy or disappointment of circumstances isn't placed on anyone, it's just a path I walk that God guides me through. I was never looking for them for anything, neither my parents, nor my birth parents, I look to God for everything. By doing this, all I have to offer them is love, because I allow God to raise me and because my sights are set on something higher. So any label that I am given by another is not defining who I am. At the core of me, is God in me, the rest of me is nothing but smoke.

DARYN WATSON

ESSAY

Learning To Stop Chasing The Reunion Carrot

MY ADOPTION REUNION IS FAST approaching its twenty year anniversary. I will always remember the first time I spoke to my birth mother in Canada. It was Monday, October 9th, 1995, Thanksgiving Day in Canada. Unlike many adult adoptees who spend years or decades searching for their biological families, my search lasted less than two months, due in part to open adoption records in Alberta, Canada.

My birth mother and I spoke for nearly ninety-minutes. Many of my questions were answered, including whom my birth father was (a distant cousin of hers). I also discovered I had two younger brothers she had with her long time husband. Her husband knew about her relinquishing me, however, her other sons were completely unaware of their elder brother.

I had always dreamed of having a brother. My parents had a daughter and my Mom had a rough pregnancy: including *seventy-eight hours* of labor only to give birth to a breach baby. That was the main reason as to why my Mom decided to adopt a boy.

Throughout the years, I've witnessed several daytime talk shows highlighting first time reunions between a birth parent and the son or daughter they relinquished many years earlier. In almost all of the cases— I was brought to tears from the deep internal desire to be able to meet my birth mother. Deep down, I *wanted the fantasy* of being able to embrace my birth mother and thank her for her difficult decision to give me a better life.

Internally, I felt a deep desire for the opportunity to meet my birth mother and to begin a relationship with my newfound brothers. I introduced the idea of spending Christmas with my birth mother's family.

They agreed (I got a blessing from my adoptive family).

In hindsight, I would do things very differently. There was plenty of happiness at the beginning of the trip but there was a lot of tension as well. I felt sorry for my birth mother's husband as he felt threatened by the attention I was getting from my birth mother as we tried to "catch up" on the lost years. Those years can never be recovered but they can, and in my opinion, need to be grieved.

Some of the mistakes I made with our initial reunion were assuming my brothers and I would automatically form a strong bond. I assumed my brothers would accept me into their lives immediately and unconditionally. How naïve I was to believe that there would not be any resistance to me entering their lives without any aftermath. The nearly two-thousand miles journeyed between my birth family's home in southern Alberta and my place (Austin, TX).

Since my maternal brothers had no prior knowledge of me— they didn't have any opportunity to think about an older half-brother somewhere out in the world. Because of this, I believe, was a contributing factor to us not having any direct or consistent contact to that day. There are several other potential factors involved as to why we don't have contact.

I can only surmise from what I have observed with my reunion experience.

For the first fourteen years of my reunion with my maternal family, I did not have any contact with anyone in my paternal family. Both my birth mother and I had written to my birth father but I never got a response. I was becoming more curious as to what, if anything, my paternal brothers knew about me.

I used Facebook to search for my potential brothers living in southern Alberta. I found who I thought could be my brother named Aaron Friedley. With some trepidation, I sent him a friend request. A couple of days later, he wrote and asked how we knew each other.

"Oh, man, I have to tell him the story" of my birth mother and "our" father. I hope he doesn't reject me"

I thought. I proceeded to tell him about my birth mother and his father and what happened that one fateful night in the back seat of our father's car in October, 1969. I think I ended the story with "I believe that we are brothers" and I sent my reply.

Surprisingly, a couple of days later Aaron accepted my friend request. He wrote me that Sunday, informing me there had been a lot of unique and crazy things in his family growing up so he wasn't that too surprised about my existence. He welcomed me into the family, which was music to my ears.

I've only met Aaron once in person. It was March of 2011. Alberta had a tremendous amount of snow that winter and we arranged to meet in a city called Red Deer, Alberta, located half-way between Edmonton and Calgary. Aaron needed a ride back to the family farm and it would give us a chance to get to know each other.

After meeting his wife at the time and welcoming me into their townhome, it was time to hit the road. We connected in our personalities, the way we thought about life and sense of humor, etc. There wasn't any awkwardness between us, as if we had known each other all our lives.

He showed me the town where he grew up and we stopped at the local general store for a pit stop. As I began walking back to the rental car, I could feel the grief overwhelm my body. I had experienced and known this onslaught of emotions from the reunion with my birth mother. I also knew that it was better to let my emotions out and process them instead of stuffing them inside.

I opened the driver side door and told Aaron I needed a minute. I knelt down beside the car and began crying almost uncontrollably. "I'm so sorry" I told Aaron, as I was sure he must have been very uncomfortable with me and my freezing crocodile tears. With grace and compassion he replied "It is okay. I don't know what you must be going through— but it is okay."

I was so grateful for his reply and ability to give me space to grieve in front of him without judging me. After a couple of minutes, I wiped my tears away and we continued on our journey to the family farm.

We spent three hours together that day but those three hours were incredible to me. I finally felt a connection with a brother that I had only dreamed of having throughout my life. Aaron and I stay in touch via Facebook and the occasional phone call. Unfortunately, our other attempts to see each other since that day have not worked out. But I know I can count on Aaron's love, respect and support.

If there is one thing I could tell adoptees in reunions, especially long term reunions, it's that they are complex and rarely turn out how we expect. I spent years "hoping" for a connection with my maternal brothers that never really materialized. The relationship with my birth mother has been an emotional rollercoaster and, at times, extremely draining and exhausting. I am forever grateful for meeting her and having my questions answered about why I was relinquished and spared from abuse from her father.

Sometimes, however, I think adoptees need to take a good long look and evaluate our reunions. Does the relationship with our birth family members enhance our lives or does it bring us down? I spent years thinking I could "fix" things between my birth mother and I when there would be a conflict between us.

Sometimes we could work things out but many times we could not. We would take breaks from having contact between us. Sometimes it may last a few days or weeks, but then the time between contacts became months and eventually years.

Speaking for myself, I realized I didn't *need* to have my birth mother in my life in order to live and grow. There is a huge difference between wanting someone in our lives and the co-dependent mindset of thinking we have to have a person in our lives in order to validate our own existence. I would question myself "Am I doing the right thing by staying in contact with my birth mother or should I let go of the relationship?"

A friend once loaned me a cassette tape with a talk by the therapist named "Terry Gorski." I don't remember the name of the talk but it was on relationships. I will attempt to paraphrase what Terry said:

"If you have a relationship where one person is a 10 (high functioning) and one person is a 2 (low functioning), you don't have a relationship that is a five or a six. You have a relationship that is a 2. A relationship cannot rise above the level of the lowest functioning person in a relationship."

This resonated with me to my inner soul. I thought about this dynamic between my birth mother and me. I am not saying I am a ten and she is a two, but I felt in many ways, I functioned at a higher level than she was capable of doing. This new perspective helped me to realize that I could continue with my life with or without my birth family involved. I wasn't *dependent* on my birth mother's acceptance or approval to be able to be whole.

It has taken me a lot of therapy, processing and years to realize that I am my own person. My journey to becoming more complete inside continues. I still have to cope with things in my life that are challenging because of being traumatized at birth through the relinquishment process of adoption. But now I am *aware* of why I get triggered and have a sense of how to deal with things as they arise.

Adoptees are usually more likely to desire contact and an ongoing reunion with birth family members than our birth families want to have contact with adoptees. That is a hard pill to swallow for many adoptees in reunions, myself included. But if we can learn to let go of expectations of our birth families and how we think the reunions should go, we can be free inside our own skin.

ANNEGHEM WALL

POETRY

(m)other

there is always something within the nothingness
a womb, waiting to be filled through carelessness
a life in the silence

the first wrench of separation
enough to wound permanently...clever Dr Winnicott said
"there is no such thing as an infant, only infant and mother"
the symbiotic entanglement of another
never was and never can be:
you said
that when your mother found out, she beat you with a wooden coat hanger
whilst I, 5 months gestating, suspended
eyes gummed shut
held on

you said
that as soon as you had birthed, the midwife cleaned off the vernix and secreted me away,
head sheltered from you, cradled into her breast
thinking that if you couldn't see me, you couldn't fall in love
but at least they gave you a photo, a facsimile of our incubation

all these years, they have passed by like water
and I still do it you know?
I stay invisible
so that no one can love me, because if they dared
I run and I run: scared
afraid of the weight of the connection
the expectations that I can only ever fail to meet
petrified of the threat of loss
because every one, lights the touch paper of the first

the most profound
the one that left me void, I avoid
because the chasm is inexhaustible, its voracious and unrelenting desire to be filled
but with what?
the pills?
the burns and cuts?
running away from the grief,
relief
each experience a barometer
which one day might swing to 'real'

taking back my story, I stop apologising
and
the edges gilded and reworked,
grow
as solid as a cast iron weight
anchored to hope

GRACE NEWTON

ESSAY

From Adopted To Adoptee

FOR A LONG TIME, THE word "adopted" was simply an adjective used to describe myself; it was not until recent years that I began to incorporate my adoption as an integral part of my being. Like for many young people, college has been a time of significant change and personal growth. For me personally, the change I have experienced in regards to my identity – specifically as an adopted person has been particularly profound.

With college, I entered a large community of adoptees, gaining not only more factual information on adoption, but also a support network of people with whom I share a similar history. I stood in awe of the artists, performers, and scholars around me. Moreover, I admired their confidence and intimate knowledge of self. It was only after reflecting on the narratives they told and connecting them to my own that I stopped referring to my adoption as a passive event from my past— but consciously acknowledged its continuous influence in my life. I thus transformed from adopted to an adoptee.

I had always hesitated to emphasize my adoption for three unequivocal reasons. First, it was already made obvious when standing beside my Caucasian parents. Second, I was (and am) a relatively shy person in unfamiliar settings and wanted to minimize the unwanted attention. And third, my adoption had previously been a source of exclusion served alongside discomforting questions and infuriating ignorance.

In contrast, taking on the title of adoptee has been a point of connection and has opened up a new world to me – one that I never knew existed before. The relationships I've created within the adoptee community have been some of the fastest and deepest I've experienced thus far. Though sometimes separated by age, race, and place, these friendships have been continuously fostered through discussions, conferences, and online engagement.

November of 2014 marked an expansion of even more adoptee connections for me. With the Twitter hashtag, and social media movement, #FlipTheScript, I found a steady stream of adoptees' thoughts on adoption, gender, class, race, and all the intersections in between them. I constantly checked for new ideas and nodded in virtual agreement to many of the posts. When I began to share my own #FlipTheScript tweets, I realized that with the click of a button, my blip of a thought joined the stack of other adoptees' tweets. And together, our compiled voices were being heard. #FlipTheScript was monumental for me because it was the first time that I felt not only a part of a wonderful community, but part of a larger movement.

Through adoption, other people made life-altering decisions on my behalf when I was first taken to the Nanjing Children's Welfare Institute, when it was decided that I would go to America, and when my adoptive parents and thus new life were chosen for me. The beginning of my life, and so many adoptees' lives, can be characterized by a complete lack of control. Changing my language to describe myself as an adoptee instead of adopted was very much about taking back some of the power I lacked and choosing for myself how I want to identify.

In the same way that taking on the title of adoptee gave me a greater sense of agency, I think the #FlipTheScript movement was about raising our voices together and taking back power in a larger sense. Through these three simple words, we showed that we are not only choosing our collective identity, but what we want to do with that identity.

For too long, other people have told adoptees how we should feel, what we should think, and in what ways we should act. We have been asked time and time again to take a back seat in regards to our own lives. No longer letting others decide what the adoption experience means, #FlipTheScript was a way of defining that for ourselves. Through the #FlipTheScript movement, we stressed the need to flip the current expectations on adoptees. We sought to change the one-dimensional, simplified adoption stories that are widely told, and to make our truths known using various Medias.

It was so exciting when #FlipTheScript left the internet and started permeating news stations. Moreover, seeing my friends, peers, and role models speaking out on behalf of the adoptee community and themselves filled me with a greater sense of pride about being an adoptee than I had ever experienced before. While I would have previously stated that I was proud to be an adoptee, #FlipTheScript helped me clearly articulate the reason behind this. Being an adoptee is hard at times, yet it's something that I live out on a daily basis. I'm proud of having a clear sense of myself despite not knowing any grounding facts about my first few years. I'm proud of being able to gracefully navigate uncomfortable situations regarding race and my family's formation. I'm proud to belong to a community of such dynamic, inspirational people dedicated to change – and I hope to join their ranks someday.

National Adoption Awareness Month only comes once a year, but the movement lives on. Through pursuing further opportunities in which we can come together and raise our voices, we continue to #FlipTheScript to reflect our own realities. While the change may be slow and the process may long, the adoptee community has shown me over and over the importance of resilience. It's a lesson we've had to learn from a young age, and it's a lesson we continue to learn when our truths are met with contention. I am confident, however, that we will keep speaking and keep pushing back until the change we seek is finally realized.

SARAH ELIZABETH GREER

ESSAY

Bio-Hazard:
A *RELATIVE* COMODY

WHILE MOST BABIES, AFTER THEY are born, go home with the person who gave birth to them— I ended up going home with an Amish family. And during that time, my name was Amy Yost. Luckily, that lasted only for three months. Then I was transferred to the Greers...where I became a bonafide *Greer Whisperer.*

It was just like being a dog whisperer, a horse whisperer or a ghost whisperer, where you are actually understanding and communicating with an entirely different species or entity from your own in another-worldly way— but instead of being dogs, horses or ghosts— it was other humans who carried completely different genes than me. They were wired differently. But that didn't stop me from "Nancy Drew-ing" my way through their labyrinth of biological falderal, where I prided myself on being able to detect and decipher ALL the psychological and emotional nuances of *my* family of Greer: John, Connie and Jonathan, the three greatest loves of my life, forever and ever, till death do us part. We were a family and we belonged together, like the Four Musketeers. My stakes were as high as a Greer Whisperer, that if hyper-vigilance and loyalty were Olympic events— I would have taken the gold.

The definition of Hyper-Vigilance is this: "An enhanced state of sensory sensitivity accompanied by an exaggerated intensity of behaviors whose purpose is to detect threats."

In short, the only two words you need to remember here are: EXAGGERATED INTENSITY. That's me in a nutshell. And it was also the way in which I dealt with my three Greers.

A TYPICAL EVERYDAY SCENARIO:

I remember the time when I was at my friend Michelle Lewis's house, and she invited me for dinner. So I called home to ask permission. My father answered. When I asked him if I could stay, he said something that sounded very alarming to me. He said, "Let me go and ask your mother, *she's taking a nap.*" OH MY GOD, SHE WAS TAKING A NAP! I got all bent out of shape. My stomach felt like it was going to explode and my chest started to hurt. I thought to myself, WHY would my mother be taking a nap? I concluded that she must be sick. Or worse. Depressed. OH MY GOD, SHE WASN'T HAPPY. I panicked.

"Dad! What's wrong?"

"Nothing's wrong. She's tired."

'I DON'T BELIEVE YOU!" I screamed, "IF EVERYTHING IS OKAY, HOLD THE PHONE UP TO HER MOUTH AND TELL HER TO SAY: *EVERYTHING'S OKAY*!"

So, he took the phone back to my mother — he was practically running with it, I could hear him bump into the wall in the hallway in all his frenzy and wince in pain, but he reached her in record time, out of breath and totally worked up. She was snoozing peacefully on the sofa. He shook her.

"Connie…Connie…*Is everything okay?*"

She woke at once and scolded him.

"Johhhhn, why did you wake me up?"

"Sarah's worried about you."

I heard her sigh out of frustration and then she yelled, "I AM TAKING A CAT NAP!"

I felt nuts. I was on the floor of the Lewis's kitchen at this point, nursing a nosebleed and reeling with nausea and a sense of impending doom. Mrs. Lewis was on the floor with me, holding tightly to my hand. From the way I was acting, she convinced herself that my mother must have had a heart attack or been in a terrible accident.

I shouted, "Dad! Ask her the question!"

"WHAT QUESTION, SARAH?"

"IF EVERYTHING IS *TRULY* OKAY WITH MOM, TELL HER TO SAY: *EVERYTHING'S OKAY*!"

Poor dad. He was always the go between. I could hear him bend down to speak into my mother's ear.

"Sarah wants you to say the words *"Everything's Okay"* Connie, if everything is truly okay with you and you are just taking a nap out of exhaustion instead of something more serious."

My mother knew the code.

"EVERYTHING'S OKAY!" she shouted. And just like that, my stomach stopped hurting, my worry was erased and I was free to hang up the telephone in peace and enjoy dinner with the Lewis family.

…I didn't know it back then — but most adoptees possess this quality, by the way. It is a trait most often linked to Post Traumatic Stress Disorder.

I loved my mother sooo MUUCH. I would do anything to make her happy. Thing was, she was so extremely practical and no nonsense, that most days she couldn't tolerate my everyday antics. She couldn't. We were wired differently. A hen just cannot understand the inner workings of a monkey. So. In an effort to appease her, I became a servile, self-abnegating and ingratiating perfectionist. I won awards and starred in my high school plays. I went to bible school and memorized verses. I joined 4-H and learned how to cross stitch and even made her a pillow.

But just as a leopard can't change its spots, there came a day when I was fired from my job as a wench at the PA Renaissance Faire for diving head first into the mud pit. I had been dared by one of the mud beggars to take the plunge in full costume, and had been fired on the spot. When I came home covered head to toe in mud and told my mother what had happened, she became apoplectic. She screamed, "Sarah! You wonder why people think of you as "el weirdo" and I'm telling you it's because you have no credibility! None! People don't take you seriously because you don't take yourself seriously! You have no credibility, kid!"

Out of curiosity, I looked up "credible" in the Random House Dictionary, and this is what it said:

Credible: "1. Capable of being believed; believable. 2.
Worthy of belief or confidence; trustworthy."

It hit me hard that my mother thought I had no credibility – but she had a point. Because when I really thought about it, deep down I had always felt very low self worth. How could I be worthy of belief? I was invisible. I wasn't real. I was adopted. And I HATED myself because of it.

And at those moments, the lowest of the low moments when I truly hated myself— I secretly thought of HER. My biological mother. I never wanted to meet my Bio. EVER. Ewwwww. Why would I? As far as I was concerned, my biological mother was nothing but a sad and sorry loser – who probably also smoked cigarettes! And I had asthma. So. THANK GOD I was being loved and raised by the Greers. Every night I would get down on my knees and thank God for them. They were my precious angels, and I knew that nothing, ABSOLUTELY NOTHING could EVER come between us or change the close-knit, safe and solid alliance we had with one another.

...AND THEN SHE FOUND ME.

My first instinct here is to just throw back my head and bellow an anguished scream of sorts; a primal call of other-worldy recognition, a laugh mixed with a cry so loud and obnoxious and full of layers of such grief and complexity and raw passion that if you were to hear it, it would scare you— then throw myself on the ground and throw bucket after bucket of water over my head, like libations, just like Electra did in Aeschylus's The Libation Bearers.

Oh. Turns out I'm Greek.

And it was Aeschylus who once said:

"He who learns must suffer, and, even in our sleep, pain that cannot forget falls drop by drop upon the heart, and in our own despair, against our will, comes wisdom to us by the awful grace of God."

THE TOP THREE FACTS ABOUT BEING FOUND BY MY BIO

#1. Nature called – and I answered the call. Literally. The very first time I heard my biological mother's voice was at 8 pm on the telephone on January 12, 1991. I remember this date – because oddly enough, it had been *her* birthday. What irony. I didn't expect to recognize her voice – but I did. Well...my cells did. As an adoptee, it was my very first experience of being able to understand things on a cellular level. Turns out I was wired to remember her voice, her zany humor, her over-the-top wild woman essence. It's the thing I came here to the planet with, too. I was having my very first neurobiological connected conversation – and the only way I can even begin to try and translate its effects are to compare it to what it must be like when deaf people can suddenly hear or blind people can suddenly see. And it exhilarated me. It changed what I knew to be real. It upended my sanity in ways. It devastated me.

#2. My biological mother's name is Susan Mastros Dohner. And yes, you are right about the pronunciation of her last name. It is pronounced DONOR. (My father's response? "Thank God it's not Donner!") She fell in love with my biological father at the age of twelve, and one night when they were fifteen and sixteen and still in high school, they got hot and heavy while watching The Man With a Thousand Faces, starring Lon Chaney— and I was conceived. That was a horror movie. And it was the very first time they ever had sex. My biological mother didn't tell anyone she was pregnant until one week before I was born. The first time she showed me my birth certificate, under the heading Traits of Biological Mother were the typed words, *"A bit of a show off"*.

#3. The very first time I MET MY MAKER was on March 30, 1991. I remember this date, because it was the day before Easter Sunday, the day symbolizing Jesus Christ's resurrection from the dead. And now, it also symbolized mine. Because on the day that I met my biological mother for the first time and looked into her eyes, a death took place. It was the death of me as I had adapted myself to be, and everything that came before. And then I arose from the dead and was reborn. I became real.

There was one thing about my biological mother that set her apart from ANYONE I had ever met before in my life: she was hysterically funny, a bang your hands on the table at all times hilarious clown. I want to tell you – I have laughed before. But this funny was different somehow. This funny was sensational. She was a totally outrageous woman and we were kindred spirits. We both found that we fell to the floor in the same way when we laughed. We shared the same mannerisms, the same over-the-top absurdity and the same sense of making magical moments out of the ordinary. I've never done drugs... but, being with her felt like being on drugs. And I couldn't get enough. I was in love. Which to me— didn't seem natural.

Out of curiosity, I looked up the word *natural* in the Random House dictionary and was totally surprised to find a definition with some "inside humor" attached.

> **Natural: "1. As is normal or to be expected; ordinary or logical. 2. Not supernatural or strange. 3. Not adopted but rather related by blood."**

HAHAHAHA!!! What a riot.

Not.

Meeting my biological mother had interrupted the natural order of things – and, in a sense everything I knew to be natural— injecting me and my parents with a newfound incomprehensible and unspeakable loss. OF EACH OTHER!!!

My mother's reaction was to make Hyper-Vigilance her game, too.

A TYPICAL EVERYDAY SCENARIO:

One day my mother called me at 7 in the morning in a panic to inform me that she was watching The Today Show, and she saw that New York City was in the middle of a huge electrical storm.

"UN-PLUG YOUR TV AT ONCE," she shouted, "IN CASE LIGHTNING STRIKES INSIDE YOUR APARTMENT!"

She sounded like I do when I have an allergy attack – she was wheezing and breathing heavily.

"YOUR SPACE IS JUST SO SMALL, HONEY, THAT I'M AFRAID THE LIGHTNING MIGHT HIT YOUR TV AND CATCH YOUR RUG ON FIRE – AND THEN YOUR WHOLE APARTMENT WILL BURN DOWN!"

Thus, our new life had begun.

For several years, I was in total shock. All I could do was mourn. All I could see was the tragedy. Being found out-of-the-blue had been a call to action – I knew that – but I became paralyzed in my grief. It was the beginning of my Hero's Journey, but instead of looking for a way to surrender to it all and accept what was now true and move forward, all I could do was resist. I just couldn't accept that everything had changed – disappeared. Instead, I made it my mission to instead try and chase answers to deeply existential questions. WHY had I been found? WHY would I hurt and betray John and Connie Greer, my two greatest loves, by embracing the bios in my life? WHY was the biological connection so earth shattering? WHY was I sabotaging my life? And on and on and on. Forget about a career – I was BUSY. My job was to find out WHY. So I went on a 20-year spiritual quest. I waited tables, researched, wrote, explored and mourned.

At one point I thought I was going insane. So, in an effort to help myself, I made an appointment to see the head of psychiatry at Columbia University. While sitting across from this woman and WAILING about my WHY's for four hours, she sat behind her desk completely straight-faced and took copious notes. When I was through with my story, she stared at me, dumbstruck, for a very long time. And THEN – after handing her $650.00 in cash, she handed me the piece of paper she had been writing on, and along with various names of medications she had listed as possibilities with lots of question marks after each medication, she had drawn a circle and inside the circle she had written: *Funny. Is her mania a symptom of mental illness – or is it just part of her personality?*

I started to study the art of comedy. One night I was in a comedy class at Stand-Up NY for women comediennes. The teacher was a recovering alcoholic, and ran his comedy classes like an AA meeting. He said, "Ladies, you are only as sick as your secrets." And then he instructed us one by one to get up on the comedy stage and reveal a deep, dark secret about ourselves. Every woman who got onstage revealed something horrifying about herself; that she had been a victim of an unreported date rape or had been participating in an incestuous relationship with a family member for several years or had once burned her house down as a child...the list of outrageous hellish secrets was endless. But what struck me was how moving and powerful each woman's personal story was, and how electric the energy in the room became and how in each tragedy, there was indeed comedy that was raw and priceless and authentic. When it was my turn I got up and blurted out, "I'm adopted!" I don't know how to describe what happened next; I started weeping uncontrollably and I fell to my knees like only an over-the-top Greek drama queen can, and out of my mouth came all sorts of crazy confessions about my life with the Greers and the Bios and how it felt to be adopted. All I can say is...the women were screaming with laughter as I let loose and poured my heart out, the whole truth and nothing but the truth. And the more they laughed – the more I shared. The whole thing lasted for about fifteen minutes, and when I finished, I got a standing ovation. It was a shamanic experience, because I learned about the power of sharing a tragic story in a funny way. Strangely I felt healed, and understood to my core in that moment that it wasn't going to be anti-depression medication that was going to heal me...it was laughter! LAUGHTER TRULY WAS THE BEST MEDICINE .

That was it. I knew what my game in life was going to be: To use the power of storytelling and humor to write and perform a comedy about the tragedy of adoption – part stand-up comedy, part art installation mixed with image and text.

I became hell-bent.

Between 1999 and 2001, I crafted and performed the stories of *BIO-HAZARD* as part of a solo performance workshop at the Westbeth Theatre Center, NYC. In November 2001, I performed the work as part of Ensemble Studio Theatre's *Oktoberfest*. That same year I mounted it as a 90-minute work-in-progress during the *HA! Comedy Festival*. The stories continued to be told in a variety of small downtown New York venues over the next few years, which led to 2, 2.5-hour staged readings in September 2005 as part of the Artists of Tomorrow Series produced by Six Figures Theatre Company, NYC. In 2009 I performed a version of *BIO-HAZARD* every other Monday night in March, April and June at The Peoples Improv Theater to sold-out crowds. The show climaxed with a surprise appearance by my biological mother, who joined me onstage for a baton twirling routine and to teach the audience a Greek dance.

Having my biological mother appear in my show was life-altering and brought about a new vision for the show: to call it BIO-HAZARD: (a relative comedy)— and then invite BOTH of my mothers to join me onstage to help me perform it! I didn't want my show to just be about *my* transformation – I wanted it to be about the transformation of *both* of my mothers as well. I wanted to create a piece of theatre where all three of us would take a stand for each other in a way that would show others that love is stronger than fear and stronger than shame. I envisioned it as a powerful, one-of-a-kind reality show; a veritable *show-and-tell* where the audience would get to experience both sides of nature and nurture up close and personal.

The thing was – I didn't have any money. I had produced all of my past shows on waitressing tips alone. So I became bold and created a Kickstarter Campaign and raised $18,000.

I wrote a new incarnation of the script, which was a comic re-telling of the Persephone/Demeter myth, and asked both mothers if they would appear as my Greek chorus in togas. Miraculously, they said yes. Once I had their promise that they wouldn't back down at the last minute, I entered my script into the International United Solo Festival, which is the largest solo festival in the world. One hundred solo shows— 50 men and 50 women from around the world, are chosen. My script was accepted and slated to debut on November 13th, 2012.

I was scared half to death, but worked around the clock to make my vision happen. Because of my Kickstarter money, I was able to hire an incredible team of artists to help make my vision happen. I hired an animator, a video artist, a choreographer for the mothers, a stage manager and a successful New York director. I bought a new projector and screen. I hired a costume designer to create costumes for my mothers. I bought a spinning base drum.

On the night of the big show, my two mothers got in a circle before the show like old pro's and did their warm-up exercises and laughed at each other's costumes. I was exhilarated beyond words that the three of us had the opportunity to be onstage together. And once the show started, we had a ball. I became my friend that night, I let go of all of the hesitation and apology that had been living inside of my heart and just connected with my audience.

Five days later, I was informed that my play had won BEST COMEDY of the festival!

Performing with both my birth mother and my adoptive mother on that magical night symbolized my AWAKENING to my spiritual connection to the universe. I will never be able to express my gratitude to the both of them for their once-in-a-lifetime gift to me. TOGETHER we were making meaning of our lives and our experience in the adoption triad. TOGETHER we were experiencing wholeness and interconnectedness. Pretending onstage together was not just a form of play – it was imagined possibility. So TOGETHER we were imagining the possibility of an intimate and fun connection and showing the audience that when a new possibility is created, reality shifts.

It is my belief that my life lesson has been to see and embrace the bigger picture of our earthly destiny, which is to see that everybody has a mortal family, true. And to see my adoption as a gift, because I have had the great fortune to have two mortal families – one that contains my nurture and one that contains my nature. Aaaaand, that if I wouldn't have been metaphorically abducted by aliens in the first place and then tested on every level by then experiencing my neurobiological connection to my birth mother, I would never have experienced the life lesson to look beyond my mortal family experience to the cosmic family experience OUT OF NECESSITY to embrace the idea that all of us are connected, that as human beings we are all one universal family. Telling my story on a stage makes my life bigger and allows me to connect.

Now I perform the show solo, without my mothers on the stage with me. Their presence in my art is now only virtual – but both of them are with me every single time I step on the stage. And it feels WONDERFUL to have found a home for my heart in the theatre, intimately connecting with my universal family.

Without being adopted, I would never have found my purpose. And since I've found my purpose, I understand this motto with my whole soul: BE WHO YOU WERE MEANT TO BE.

Now I make up my own definitions these days. Like this one:

**ECCENTRIC: 1. One that deviates markedly from an established norm, especially
a person of odd or unconventional behavior. 2. To be whimsical, outlandish,
a bit daft, wacko. Have a moon-flaw in the brain, have a screw loose.**

Those definitions were taken from the dictionary. But this next one's all mine. I created it myself.

**ECCENTRIC:
3. A person who follows their higher path.**

162

MEI-MEI AKWAI ELLERMAN, PHD
ART

SHANNON GIBNEY

ESSAY

Losing Sianneh, Losing Patricia

PRELIMINARY REMARKS

WHENEVER MOTHER AND CHILD LOSE each other, it is a tragedy. Whether through adoption, death, or some other form of separation, the loss is both primary and secondary — it paralyzes when it happens, but the body and spirit remember the drowning ache of it throughout life, in spirals, sometimes in a new place, when you think it would never visit, and even when you don't recognize its face.

Of course, no one wants to hear about loss on this scale ——not really. Not in our culture, where success is measured in how many times you can smile and cheerfully persevere through difficulty. Difficulty in the service of overcoming is one thing. Difficulty in the service of its own sake, in the service of recognizing the horrific that can come in daily life is another thing entirely.

WHO

wants to wake in terror? To not be able to reach for that flesh that is safety? To be homeless…at least for a time, which can feel like an eternity to the uninitiated?

To be baptized in loss, is, after all, to be christened living with a hole in your heart. To go through your life wheezing through the lack, all the while gasping for that elusive full breath.

THIS IS WHAT IT MEANS TO BE ALIVE

What it has always meant to be alive.

And yet, only some of us are alive.

WHEN WE LOST HER

it seemed that I would never have to explain anything again. Why I sometimes fall into melancholy. The single scream in the hospital bathroom. Her fuzzy gray shoes that her brother had picked out, so irrelevant, on the dresser.

She had stopped breathing. Her heart had stopped for some reason at forty-one and a half weeks. No one knew why. No one will ever know why.

WHEN I LOST HER

they had pulled me out with Forceps. She did hold me, but her hands shook. She did not recognize me, nor I her. The doctor did not speak, the nurse did not smile. No one knew my name, except that I was Lost. Lost in the world. So blurry.

There was a reason for this. It was unfortunate, but necessary. Everything that has happened to me since has been necessary.

WHEN A THING IS BROKEN

can it ever be broken again? Rebroken into something new, or what it was before?

CONCLUDING REMARKS

I have tried to make something of a relationship with my birth mother. It has not worked. I think it is a combination of too much time, and too many truths that defy definition. That and the fact that we do not understand each other's languages.

I have not tried to talk to my dead daughter yet. Some day, I intend to. There are things I need her to hear. There are also things I need her to hear me say to her. Not to explain, but to be a witness for each other.

To mark this leaving...on and on.

But not to dread it.

JULIE STROMBERG

Essay

Sex, Lies and Adoption

THE FIRST TIME I VISITED Baltimore's historic Charles Theater was in the fall of 1989. At 18-years-old, I had just arrived in town to begin my freshman year at Loyola College. A new friend joined me for a showing of Stephen Soderbergh's film *Sex, Lies, and Videotape*. Sitting in the dark theater, I had no idea at the time that this formative part of my life's script would set into motion my own journey of self-discovery as an adoptee.

I found myself back at the Charles Theater in the fall of 2013. This time, it was for a showing of *Philomena*, a British drama film based on the book *The Lost Child of Philomena Lee* by journalist Martin Sixsmith. Both the book and the film depict the story of Lee and the son she lost to adoption.

THE CONFLICT

Lee's story is one with which many of us involved in adoption policy reform are familiar. As an 18-year-old in 1950s Ireland, Lee became pregnant. Disowned by her strict Catholic family, she joined the thousands of single, pregnant Irish women sent to Catholic Church operated convents during the 1950s and 1960s. Lee ended up at the Sean Ross Abbey which was operated by the Sacred Heart Sisters in Roscrea in County Tipperary. According to Mike Milotte's book *Banished Babies: The Secret History of Ireland's Baby Export Business*, 438 babies born at Sean Ross were secretly sent to America for adoption. Lee's son was one of those babies.

The film presents Lee's story as it unfolds after she becomes acquainted with the journalist Sixsmith and the two embark on a search for her lost son soon after his 50th birthday. Judi Dench is superb as the elder Lee and Steve Coogan gives life and humor to the cynical Sixsmith character. The relationship between the two is a highlight of the film and brings a sense of lightness to what is truly a poignant and heart-wrenching tale. In fact, relationships are the key theme of the film. While the atrocities endured by Lee and other young women are depicted and acknowledged, the heart of the story is in Lee's own heart as a mother who feels a deep connection to the son who lived at the convent with her until he was three-years-old. As an adoptee and a viewer, I liked this aspect of the film very much. I liked that the focus was on Lee's deep love for her son and how she never once stopped thinking of him or searching for him. This film offers a reminder that the connection between parent and child can rise above even the most horrific of circumstances.

Certain aspects of the film also mirrored some of my own experiences with Catholic institutions as a domestic American adoptee who was adopted through Catholic Charities as an infant in 1971. In the film, we learn that Lee visited the Sean Ross Abbey on several occasions with the hope of finding out what had become of her son. We also learn that as an adult, her son had also visited the convent with the hope of learning more about his mother. The convent nuns never tell one about the other, despite having the information readily available and having engaged in discussions with both.

THE BACK STORY

My natural father first visited Catholic Charities of Fairfield County in 1989, around the time that his 18-year-old daughter was sitting in a Baltimore city movie theater watching actor James Spader point a video camera at actress Andie MacDowell. His intent was to inquire about me and make all of his information available. The Catholic Charities social worker would not tell him anything about me—not even my birth date. But she did tell him that, for a fee, he would be allowed to fill out paperwork containing all of his information. He was then informed that if I ever contacted the agency, his details would be provided to me. My father wrote out the check, completed the forms and began searching for his only child.

In 1998, at the age of 27, I did contact Catholic Charities of Fairfield County to inquire about my natural parents and learn what I could about my background. The same social worker who worked with my father years earlier spoke with me. She never mentioned that my father had released his information to me. But she did say that if I were to pay a $250 fee, Catholic Charities would conduct a search for me. I opted to keep my checkbook closed.

Fortunately, my father and I found each other through ISRR. After we reunited, my father told me about how he had released his information and asked if the agency had provided it to me. No, they did not, I confirmed. Then, seeing as Catholic Charities had no idea that my father and I had found each other, I decided to make an inquiry. I sent a letter requesting that any information left for me by either of my parents be provided as soon as possible.

A week later, I received a phone call from the same social worker who had worked with both my father and me. She informed me that Catholic Charities had good news and bad news. The good news, she said, was that my father had released all of his information to me years earlier. The bad news, she then explained, was that the agency could not release it without my mother's permission—because she was considered the agency's client (please note that as the actual former "child in need," the agency does not consider me, one of its adoptees, to be a client). My father was not informed of these details when he paid his fee in 1989. To this day, I have never been provided with the information that Catholic Charities promised my father it would release.

THE RESOLUTION

While watching the film and considering my own personal experience, I couldn't help but reflect on the lack of compassion offered to the natural parents, sons and daughters of adoption by some global Catholic institutions. Some of these actions occurred not only in the 1950s, but in the 1990s and 2000s. So this is not a matter of "oh well, that was a long time ago." In one sense, Catholic Charities of Fairfield County in Connecticut did to my father and the adult me what the Sean Ross Abbey nuns in Ireland did to Philomena and her adult son—withheld vital information, lied by omission and intentionally kept us from one another.

This script is in need of a major rewrite.

SUSAN HARRIS O'CONNOR, MSW

ESSAY

A Racial Bouquet:
DISCUSSING ADOPTION AND MY RACIAL IDENTITY THEORY

To my mothers, Toby Judith Klayman and the late, Dorothea Rae Harris
Both of you have contributed immeasurably, yet, in such different ways, in helping me
to become a full functioning person who believes she has purpose and meaning.

I WAS IN THE THROES OF deep suffering following the death of my adoptive mother in 1989. Until then, I had functioned well, lived and held my adoption status rather naively. Placing it within the framework of a word that helped to simplify the circumstances of my life's beginnings and the obvious racial differences between me and my white adoptive parents and white siblings. I understood adoption in a rather non-dimensional way. I knew I was adopted; I knew that I was transracially adopted, but I didn't know what that really meant in terms of my identity or the impact it had had on my existence.

When my adoptive mother died, I immediately found myself in a place of unspeakable and incomprehensible emotional and psychological pain. It felt as if I were as close to being dead as one could be while knowing that they were alive. Within what appeared to be a moment, I became a shell of a person. I became nothing. My favorite person in the world, the woman I adored and counted on to be there for me was gone, and most of me, quite frankly, had gone with her.

For many years, I viewed myself as being rather non-functional. Experiencing the overwhelming multi-dimensionalness of being transracially adopted while grieving my adoptive mother. Adoption, transracial adoption were no longer just simple terms. Even if I wanted them to be, they couldn't be. There was no longer an ability to speak of adoption or race in a rather blasé' way. I could no longer hold these areas narrowly or speak of these issues in light, meaningless ways. My adoptive mother's death forced me into the depths of my identity as a transracial adoptee. I could no longer deny the need to know the mother who birthed me; the mother who was with me when I took my first breath. I needed her, more than ever. I needed to connect, to racially belong. I was struggling, and rightfully so.

When I began writing autobiographical narratives in 1996 their etiology was coming from a place of transracial adoptee isolation and loss. Each narrative assisted me in my healing journey in ways in which traditional treatment could not. They profoundly impacted me. However, in 1999 after a six month in-depth study of my racial and cultural identity, it was my fourth performance narrative

The Harris Racial Identity Theory: Reflections of a Transracial Adoptee that would change forever my understanding of racial and cultural identity. It is this narrative that would assist in re-defining society's understanding of racial identity; particularly in the area of transracial adoption.

Due to my racial classification that emphasized me being both Black and white, I was viewed as being an undesirable baby in 1963. When I took on the task of studying this part of me, what I found initially interesting was thinking about why this area was so important for me to examine? There were things about me that I found boring; not worthy of mentioning. Though, just the mere thought of my racial, religious and cultural identity and how I was raised in a white community was overwhelming. The enormity of this identity, which I believe had kept me from looking at it, I realize, is what became the driving force for me to study and deconstruct it and then reconstruct it in a controlled manner. So what is this identity that would be examined?

I am a Jewish, Black, white, Native American female who was adopted across racial lines by white, Jewish parents in 1964. There it is. This is what I attempted to avoid. This is what I tried to put in a simple box. That is the identity I had, as most appeared to act like I was just like everyone else. This is my collective vulnerable identity that was seldom spoken of.

Diving into this monumental study of self, I was struck that my approach would be very different from the other self-studies and narratives I had written. I realized that I had to think more, than feel; that it would require a different way of holding the journey in order to have a chance of capturing the experience. With that understanding up front, I quickly assessed and determined that this narrative would require numerous construct categories to respectfully and honorably hold all of me. It was apparent that this racial identity was extremely complex and complicated (more so than I had ever imagined or read of in transracial adoption literature); that it was multi-dimensional, that the constructs were interwoven with fluidity; that some constructs held many experiences or identities within them. Although not exactly the correct comparison for the way in which this theory works or the way in which my racial and culturally identity exists within me; sometimes, I visualize it operating somewhat like an accordion. I had to create a model and theory that could stretch and reach with depth and width, yet, also, comfortably collapse for identities that didn't require a need to hit the high and low notes.

For me this study was about brutal honesty after having spent many years in turmoil. It wasn't about adoption or racial politics or pretending to have achieved comfort being who I was. And, it wasn't about sensationalizing the subject matter. It was about the honest truth. Regardless of what I uncovered. Regardless of how messed up it looked. Regardless of what anyone, including academics, thought.

Through deep reflection and introspection I learned that my racial identity consists of 5 racial identity constructs: genetic, imposed, cognitive, feeling and visual. These five constructs move together and hold all of me and how my racial identity is created and influenced by genetics, people, me, communities and society.

Another way I think of my racial identity is that of a beautiful bouquet of flowers in which its flowers live, breathe, and interact among each other and with its environment. Within my racial bouquet my first/birth parents gave me what I call a Genetic Racial Identity. My genetic racial identity from my birthfather is Black and Native American/Seminole Indian from Florida. I am also white, Russian, Jew through my first/birth mother. My adoptive parents had shared my racial, ethnic and religious information with me as a child.

My Imposed Racial Identity is how people label, categorize and classify me based on what they see or what they think or know me to be. Depending on one's race and ethnicity, the imposed racial or ethnic identity may allow you ongoing access and privilege. Yet, as a person of color, I view this construct as floral arrangement fillers with varying size thorns that prick and hurt as they are inserted into the human container. I was given the label negroid or Black soon after birth, even though I am genetically tri-racial; Black, white and Native. This construct also captures how I was viewed and treated because of people's racial perceptions. I realized that the imposed identity could also shift to being self-imposed. How fortunate I was to have had parents who gave me my identity information so that I knew my identity factually and could push back and say 'no' to the inaccurate identities imposed. Though, I still had to, and continue to, work through many of the internalized racial messages received.

The Cognitive Racial Identity should be the same as the genetic racial identity however this separate category is needed because although I knew factually what my genetic racial identity was, many adoptees, foster children and other people for various reasons don't have this factual identity information. This leaves them vulnerable for the imposed racial identities that are quite often inaccurate, to take control. Even though I knew racially who I was, without ever having met my birthparents or having pictures of them, added complexity which began to resolve itself once I was in reunion.

It is the Feeling Racial Identity that allows me to breathe comfortably. I feel racially white even though I am genetically Black, white and Native; even though many people view me as being Black or something other than white. This racial identity construct gives me permission to feel racially whatever I feel, regardless of whatever racial identities are imposed on me and regardless of what I am genetically. This is the area of a person's racial identity that is susceptible to being pathologized, bullied and marginalized if it doesn't line-up-to or is in-sync-with both their genetic and imposed racial identities. I had spent much of my earlier life trying to make my feeling racial identity (which is connected to my cultural identity and the way in which I was socialized), be in sync with my genetic and imposed racial identities, yet, it never happened.

The final racial identity construct within this bouquet is that of the Visual Racial Identity. It was important to me that this model acknowledges how I actually visually see the color of my skin. When I looked in the mirror I saw and continue to see a woman of color. Although my visual racial identity doesn't match my feeling racial identity; my visual racial identity isn't distorted. It accurately holds that I know that I am visibly a person of color.

I want to close by saying that once I identified these five racial identity constructs and mapped out how they had played out within me and within my environments over my lifetime, I was no longer confused by it. It's now held like a bouquet of beautifully mixed flowers and I hoping that this chapter and theory gives others the opportunity to explore and value their complex identities, similarly.

For institutions or agencies interested in scheduling a performance of the Harris Racial Identity Theory narrative, please email susan_harrisoconnor@yahoo.com.

To read the author's racial identity narrative please refer to The Harris Narratives: An Introspective Study of a Transracial Adoptee (2012). The Pumping Station

To learn more of her racial identity theory please refer to the article Ung, T., Harris O'Connor, S., Pillidge, R. (2012). The development of racial identity in transracially adopted persons: An ecological approach. Adoption and Fostering (Fall/Winter).

M. C. MALTEMPO

ESSAY

Memory May Reveal

I was crossing a large dirt field of a school in my school uniform, a poster-child for a first grader: clean uniform, light jacket, and a small yellow book bag. Maybe even a cap on my head. The morning light made shadows long but the sky was clear of clouds. The effervescence of light and dew taming the dusty dirt and the dirt's glaring out-of-place-ness, contentedness abound. This was ordinary. As I did every morning, my first grade-self was walking alone when suddenly an eagle swooped down and grabbed me by my book bag. I was snatched up by my backpack— and dragged along with it.

The eagle was in his early twenties. Skinny but not lanky. I did not recognize him. Too startled, too paralyzed, and too small to effectively protest, I could barely keep myself from falling as I was being rushed by the pull. I did not dare to make much sound. Too frightened and disoriented, I just wanted to regain my balance.

Thrown into the toilet stall, a cold shiver surged through my bones. I had not known that the portable toilet was there. I did not know what was going on and what was going to happen to me, but I felt a terrible fate was to come. Being that this is a toilet, I thought I was going to be thrown down the hole. *What did I do wrong?* He climbed into the stall with me. A peep of a sound came out of me. There was much rustling as I tried to unlatch myself from the grip of his hand. My protests were weak, meager at best. A mouse pinned by a tiger. Grabbing me with, one hand or the other, but always one hand. It was not long, possibly matter of seconds, when he had his pants down to mid-thigh. Then he pinched my ear really hard. I cringed in hot pain, burning so badly that I thought my head would explode from the pressure. Adrenaline pumping, all cylinders firing, I felt motivated. I needed to do something. Even in my effort to get away, I kept staring at it. I did not want to get peed on. Being that I was six years old, getting peed on seemed lethal. Panic set in. My heart barely contained. Sounds closing off as my pulse pumped louder. *Why is he doing this to me?* And more I pulled away from him, more my ear felt the potential tear, dismemberment. He pinched harder in response. He was rubbing his penis, his hard, erect penis. I did not know what he was doing but I was terrified. He was taller than my father. I could never challenge my father, let alone this bigger man. I began to resign to my destiny, whatever it was. Scared stiff, my world went silent as I awaited my fate.

A minute, a very long minute passed when I looked up and found a face of painful despair. He was not enjoying this, torturing me, like the evil villains in cartoons. There was something about his expression that, in hindsight, I felt sympathy for. He had to do this, no choice about it.

Before anymore sympathy could wash over me, he began to pinch harder. Something was going to happen. My hearing was returning. My awareness was quickly coming back to this toilet stall, where this tall man with a distraught, shaking face was about to kill me. I do not know how, but he was. I felt sure of it. The strain on his face and the pinch to my ear became more intense and I looked away. I braced myself. I did not know what I was bracing myself for but I wanted it over with. And I knew it was going to be very painful. He was breathing harder, exerting great effort. In complete terror, panic took over me. I felt I was burning from the inside. I thought I could jump out of my skin. He was starting to make some strained noises. I had never heard someone make such strained noises. I did not know what kind of harm was going to come my way, but the anticipation alone made me breakout in searing sweat. Then... a liquid squirted out of his penis. I flinched. He released my ear and clenched my shoulder so tightly that I thought he was going to crush it. More jelly-liquid squirted out. Again, I flinched, but this time with a breath. Then more jelly-liquid squirted out, this time with less force. I flinched a little less, but the adrenaline was still coursing through my veins, burning every bit of my body. Everything seemed still, silent and I was terrified and curious all at once. The adrenaline burned my skin, making it itch from its hot pricks. This was not painful. It was supposed to be painful. It was supposed to kill me. The devastation I anticipated was anticlimactic. My shock was quickly deflating.

But then something else, something new to fear, entered my thoughts. He was going to beat me up. He was going to beat me up and throw me down the toilet. My original fear was right. I was going to be thrown down the hole. He was going to hit me, punch me, or whip me with his penis while he was relieving himself of the pain that was contained in the liquid he expelled. I felt certain of it. But he just dripped a little more onto my jacket, on my shoulder. And his sigh of relief, which made me flinch, made him seem less dangerous all of the sudden. I was not frozen but I did not dare to move. There was not anything I could do. He was finished with me and I was evidence he did not want around. But before this thought compelled me to rebel, he put his penis away, hiked up his pants and urgently stepped backwards out of the stall with a final look. I could not decipher the look. Appreciative? Satisfied? Relieved?

The door closed.

I was alone in the portable toilet, exhausted, my eyes nearly bulging out of their sockets, my skin sizzling, electric. The jelly-liquid was on my jacket shoulder. And the look was still on my mind. *What did it mean?* I did not know how long I stayed there. It felt like a very long contemplative hour. *What just happened?* I was too scared to leave, knowing he was somewhere out there. I had to be careful.

My consciousness had awakened. There are moments in one's life when remembering and inhibiting instincts to avoid dangers keep a being alive. This was that moment.

My memory of the event is not very clear. I cannot recall if it was spring or fall, though my feelings tell me it was May. I cannot confirm if the dirt field was a school field or some other random field with my school on the other side of it. My image of the young man is of someone in his mid-twenties, but that does not reconcile with any other Asian man in his mid-twenties from my experience since then; he seemed to have acted younger but looked older.

My memory also reveals things that may not have occurred during the event but only upon my reflection of it afterward. The young man grabbed me aggressively and he dragged me to the portable toilet, which lead me to believe I was in great physical harm, but I was not roughed up. Aside from the great pacifying ear pinch, I did not take any blows. Even the pinch, I do not remember clearly; I cannot even remember which ear was pinched. This fact and the look on his face, the look of despair, the look of I-am-sorry-that-I-have-to-do-this-to-you-but-I-cannot-help-it-I-swear-I-will-be-quick-and-will-not-hurt-you-just-bear-with-me-one-moment makes me sympathize. Not that I had ever felt that way before then, but even then I felt I shared with him the sentiment that there are things in life one cannot control. I would much rather see him as an evil villain than to sympathize, but I would not be honest if I said so.

I am grateful that I was not physically harmed. But this did have two profound effects on my life. I will forever know that men have the ability and the urge to take a person hostage. As with my tormentor, now, as a grown man, I have experienced situations where I could have been him. An urge or desperation— the release of some sort of explosion that would once and for all give me peace. And I have always imagined that if such a state overwhelmed me, there would be a victim and I would somehow communicate that *I am sorry that I have to do this to you but I cannot help it; I swear I will be quick and will not hurt you; just bear with me one moment.* The other effect is one in which I will always remember the events of my life like episodes of a greater story. For this reason, I have been chronicling my life for great many years, seeking that great arc or theme or moral that drives any good story to its denouement. I want to know how I end. And it began with this awakened consciousness.

I did eventually leave the portable toilet. I had not heard anything, so, I felt safe enough to peek out. No one was there. I came out and no one was around. Seoul was one of the largest cities in the world in 1986, and yet I cannot recall the presence of a single soul that morning. I do not recall seeing a single person. I ignored the shoulder, which was not too hard since it was on the jacket and I did not feel anything. I crossed the field in a hurry. I walked into the school building and right into my classroom. Class had not yet started but the teacher was at the front of the class. I went to the bathroom to do something. I must have wanted to clean up, or check on the jacket, but I do not recall what I did. I came back to my desk, and the rest of the day was unremarkable.

After school on April 4th, I was watching television with my little brother. He was then four years old. He was a happy kid. Smiling all of the time, very bright, picked up on things and knew how to entertain adults. He and I sat on a couch; across from us was the television. Next to the television was the door to my parent's bedroom. On this particular day, the door was closed. On the other side of the door were my parents. It was mid-afternoon. My father was a DJ, working evenings and weekends. So it was not unusual for him to be around during the day. All seemed in place. No one ever seemed to have noticed my jacket; as long as it stayed this way, everything was in its rightful place. I do not recall what we were watching but my brother, easily entertained, was clearly enjoying himself. My focus, though, was on the door. Not that a bedroom door being closed was odd, and I must have seen that door closed before, but sitting on the couch, I was watching the door, not the television. I thought I heard something through the door but I was not sure. My brother laughed as heartily as a four year old could.

"I should kill you!" he roared. The bedroom door blasted open. Omma shrieked in mortal fear and fled behind the couch. Appa jumped over the couch, flipping it over, and pounced on her, grabbing her throat. Here, my memory fails me, I cannot remember what he said, but I am certain it was a lethal threat. She could not speak, air not flowing. Just when it seemed she was on the brink of collapse, he let go and stomped his way to the kitchen. She should not have been able to recover so quickly, but she did, and she grabbed Soorin with one arm and darted out.

"Omma! Omma!" I cried after her.

Appa returned with a kitchen knife, the rage was dripping out of his pores. His focus was on his wife, and seeing that she was out and had taken the children with her, he chose to stay behind. He walked into his layer. He was facing a window, steaming. He did not seem to be looking at anything in particular, that is, if he could see straight. If he was looking at something, he would have been gazing out at the horizon interrupted by the adjacent building. He seemed to be seeing something beyond what was in front of him. The man standing there was a foreigner to me. He was distant, preoccupied. He was not his usual self, engaged, charming.

Then there was a change in him. He sensed a presence. He was not alone. He knew that his family was out and yet his knowledge failed him. Through the open door behind the upturned couch a young boy ducked his head. For a moment, he was puzzled to see me. There was some calculation going on in his head that I was not privy to; at the end of which was a decision. He stomped his way over to the couch, tracing his steps over it but this time less passionately, more deliberately. He grabbed his son's hair.

"Ow, Appa! Please! What?! Appa, Appa! It hurts!" I grabbed his fist in hopes of loosening it while he dragged me around. During all of which I was staring at the weapon in the other hand. It would not take much. It would be quick. The dangerous practice I received the other day had not prepared me for staring at shining death in the face.

"You gotta go!" He dragged his son to the entry way.

"Appa, lemme have my shoes!"

"You gotta go!" He did not care about shoes.

Though I did not want to be any closer to the knife— suddenly it seemed very important to risk it all to have shoes. Even as though he was shoving me out of the door, limited by having something in his other hand, I stuck my foot out. But my bare foot was not enough for an authority three times my size, time times my senior. With a final shove, my butt hit the concrete stairs and the door slammed shut, echoes confirming.

"Appa! I'll go. Lemme have the shoes! Appa!" I was pounding on the metal door. The hollow stairway repeating back to me the useless plea I kept making. "Appa! Please! Just the shoes! I'll go with shoes!" I was answered with silence. Still I whaled in desperation, "Appaaaaa!"

I did not know how long I was pounding on the door but without shoes I had nowhere to go, so there was nothing to do but to keep trying. And, as shy as I was, I was persistent. Still, with my palm throbbing and my pleas sounding ever more meek and futile, the stairwell embarrassed me. I resigned to my barefoot destiny.

I made my way outside at some point. I did not know what I was supposed to be doing. I wondered where Omma went, and why she did not take me with her. I could not figure out what Omma could have done to enrage him so. Omma was pretty and Appa was handsome. But in one moment, Omma was a shrieking prey and Appa was an untamed carnivore. He was like an animal, completely out of control and a slave to instinct and reflex. He was visceral. He was out for blood. Pondering passed the time. There was a small playground outside of the apartment building. I went down the three floors to the ground level. I made my way across the small parking lot with no cars to the playground gravel. I did not step in it; I simply balanced on the ledge.

———

Some time passed. My memory now takes me to a movie scene. A boy stares up to an apartment. Around him is a crowd, an audience of town people, kept at bay by a few police officers. Soldiers are rappelling down the side of the building. It was cool. It was exciting. At the same time, an unsettling feeling was taking place. The rappellers were making their way to the balcony... to our balcony. And they had guns. One young soldier landed on the balcony and looked through the bedroom window. Before the other one made it onto the balcony, the first one went through the sliding door. *Was our door unlocked?* My recollection is hazy.

Some more time passed, and Omma appeared onto the scene with Soorin in her arms. She was talking to a police officer. The crowd was still staring at the balcony, awaiting some resolution. My mother had spoken to someone and gave me a pair of too-small girl's slippers to wear. I almost wanted to stay barefooted but we were going someplace and I could not possibly get very far without them.

Days passed. Omma and a bunch aunts and uncles were sitting in our living-room. Circle of elders. Only evidence of any of the previous events was on people's faces. It was a meeting of the elders. Decisions were going to be made. The adults seem to be stressed, lots of chain smoking. Buried in smoke, they were nearly speaking another language in hushed tones. I am sure my mother was among them but I cannot place her in the scene.

A decision must have been made. The result was the cold shack on a hill, our new home. I do not even recall the bathroom being attached. I think we had to go outside to an outhouse. My mother was never around, always absent and supposedly busy. I took the remaining eggs and imitated what I thought what adults did to cook them. I turned on the propane stove, put a pan on top and put the egg on the pan. Half of the egg remained stuck on the pan. I gave it to Soorin. He seemed to be hungrier than I was. The one room shack with an unheated kitchen attached to it was very isolating. I was not really missing school but I was not okay with staying home, awaiting Omma's return. Aside from constant hunger, Soorin did not seem to mind being there. He still had television. He never seemed to mind anything. Nothing fazed him. And where Omma went was unclear.

There was a whole lot that was unclear. *Why had not father allowed us back? What did the police say to him? What did Omma say that angered him so much? How was it that Soorin was so happy? Why was there no heat or hot water? Why was there no food? If we could not go back to the apartment then why can't we live with Auntie Gomo? What happened and why did it come down to this, a cold house far from everyone, and with no directions back to anything I'd ever known?*

Seoulites that were poor lived high up on the hills, small mountains, really. Seoul was a city with many hills, where their bald faces left homes to the elements. These hills were not always so bare. Most were simply not rejuvenated after the war. The desirable areas to live had been in the valleys. It had been this way for centuries. With life away from the stresses of city life, universities set up shop on these over grown hills. Other than these institutions of higher learning, people who could not afford to live among civilization lived on the hills.

I left the house to find food. I did not have any money. I had never bought anything before. Standing on the hill, I could see a good expanse of the city. I did not know that I lived with so many people. And I did not know any of them. I figured I could go down the hill and I would eventually get to somewhere I recognized. It was a sunny day and was not too cold. At first it was easy. I just had to walk downhill. Then I found myself in a labyrinth of walls, walls of stone, walls of brick, and walls of cinder-block. I could not recall how I got on the hill to begin with, so there was no retracing my steps. Now I did not know how to get off of the hill. On the other side were the city streets. Streets I could navigate. I tried this way and that. There never was a dead end. Sometimes I found myself at the same junction, which seemed completely ridiculous since I would have had to walk up hill at some point to make a circle. I had one hint that I was making progress: I was still climbing downward.

I found streets with cars and actual traffic. I made it! Only, I did not know how. I also did not know where. And I only then realized that I had not seen any people on my way down. *How was it possible that all those people lived on the hill and I would not meet or see any of them?*

The problem with Seoul was that with few exceptions everything looked familiar. Once lost, it was too easy to remain lost with the thought that the next corner will present something familiar. And that would be right. You would recognize it, whatever it was. But the thing you recognized was actually a duplicate of whatever you used to find your bearings with: a convenience store, dry cleaners, a bus stop. I was a persistent boy. I was shy to ask for help but I was not about to give up. So, I kept walking. Here and there I could see people doing their thing. There was a middle aged fat man scratching his belly and singing. There was the truck with foodstuffs being unloaded by young men wearing gloves that were dipped in red rubber and older men giving orders while smoking bent cigarettes, bent from their sweaty pockets. Then there was the entrance to some high school. A young man on a scooter with a *jjajangmyun* noodle delivery container was talking to some pretty girl in uniform, who was clearly excited to see him. She wore a pretty ribbon in her hair. He was smoking. It had been a while since I left the house but it must have been lunch time by then, otherwise the girl could not possibly be allowed to leave school grounds. I was feeling light headed. I had to keep walking, otherwise it might be too late and my father will have left to DJ at the cafe. It was not very long when I came across a section of the city completely different from what I thought was there. I was expecting something else. I cannot remember what I was expecting but I do remember that I was expecting something and I saw something completely different. This meant my mental map had a gap. But I was not too surprised, since the trek was already much longer than I thought. I decided to walk through this gap. Unlike the known sections of the city, populated with four story buildings with simple stores, food carts on the streets and neon signs for *noraebang* song rooms, this section had tall buildings. Buildings with glass and shiny stone exteriors. These buildings were so tall; they created different times of the day below in their valleys. There were no signs. People were dressed in suits, walking briskly and with purpose. Then there were the store windows. On display were such things of beauty. I did not even know what they were. I did not even really know that they were stores. There was one display that caught my eye. In it, there was another world built behind the glass. A plane— hanging from a ceiling. So high that I could not see where the string met the ceiling. A train passed by on a green carpet that was meant to resemble grass. The train moved along. There were plastic trees and cars and roads and things on trucks. There were smiling figurines: a doctor and a nurse, a fireman, a police officer and a dog. And the buildings were made with plastic bricks. One looked like a house. Another looked like a bridge. The train went by again. This time it had cargo: little brown plastic cylindrical bricks that were supposed to be logs of wood. I walked slowly and stopped to admire one detail after another. I retraced my path to admire things again. I must have looked at every detail thrice when I came to a thick glass door I had not noticed earlier. A man and his son came out through the door. The boy must have been about my age. He had a box with the picture of something that was on display. It was labeled LEGO. The father and son held hands. And I watched their backs walk away. Even their backs looked happy.

It hurt. Just the sight of him with his father—happy and holding onto his present. I pained with envy. I couldn't put it into words then but I can now. The warmth I could feel between them at that moment was strong enough to scorch its mark on me. Even to this day, recalling myself little self standing there, watching them walk away chokes me, burning my throat.

I looked into the window again. This time beyond the smiling doctor and his nurse was a scowling face. The face was looking at me. Suddenly the door opened and a woman about my mother's age stuck her head out, "Little boy, you should not stand there so long. Other people need to see." Still recovering from the awful effects of envy, I looked around, confused. There were men and women in suits walking by but no one was looking at the display, let alone appreciating its magnificence. "Why don't you come back soon with your father? Ask him to buy you that fireman with his firetruck. Okay? Go on."

I took some cautious steps back. I was hurt and now I was embarrassed. I walked across the street when I could. On the other side of the street there was a ramp. There were older kids going in and out of it. There was an old man at street level in a booth, slumping. I walked right by him, unnoticed, or he had not cared. As I descended, it was getting darker and louder. There were some teenagers walking up the ramp, chitchatting and generally having a good time, and they did not mind me any attention. So I kept going. Anxiety was building up inside me. Going deeper underground in the dark, even though there was light at the end of it all at the bottom, was making me anxious because I could not see where my feet touched the ground. And I could begin to hear squealing. The squeals were getting happier as I approached closer to the end of the ramp. And when I finally arrived at the ground, there were older boys and girls on shoes with wheels on them. They were going 'round in circles and spinning and falling and laughing and some were dancing to the beat of the music. And they were chasing each other. People were dancing, rolling their feet, hanging onto each other for support. Even when they fell, they seemed delighted by the fall. Everyone was much older than me. But no one was old.

Here my memory fails me. I do not know what happened after the dancing on wheels. I definitely made my way back out from underground to the street. I must have continued my trek toward what I thought was my old home. And at some point I had to have decided to give up and make my way back up the hill. I never reached Appa.

A stiff breeze was blowing across the street as I walked up the hill. Again I noticed that the street was empty. I finally reached the shack. I could hear that Omma was back by the sound of the television. I pulled open the door and sitting on floor pillows with partially eaten food was Omma and adorable Soorin, standing and doing something entertaining. *Was he dancing?* Omma turned her head and was immediately furious. She grabbed me by the arm, pulled me in, and closed the door behind me.

"Where were you?! I have been waiting for you for hours! Your brother was hungry so I had to cook. Why were you not home?!" She started to slap my bottom with her hand. "Where were you? Where did you go? You should not go out! Do not go out again! Never!" She continued this for a minute.

This was spanking. It did not really hurt physically. It hurt emotionally. I began to cry. Not a child's whaling cry— but a suffocated, stifled weepy cry of a child with no self-esteem. The continual pain of my mother's passionate disapproval conjured up the tears. I clenched and contorted my face to prevent an explosion. Still, hot tears leaked, streaming down my cheeks, dripping below my chin, cold by then.

"Now, go over there," she pointed to the other side of the table. There was a bowl containing a cold, sick, and congealing mass. "Eat your noodles!" *Noodles?* The noodles must have been sitting there for a very long time. Their structural integrity was not credible. Now it looked half digested. "It's cold because you were late. I bought you special ramen and now they are just cold. Eat it!" With her order, I looked at the empty bowls on the other side of the table and tried not to smell the noodle jelly soup in front of me. I put it in my mouth and it did not have the right texture. My gag reflexes activated and prevented me from getting any of it down. I bit off a little of the noodles but I started dry heaving. "It's all of your fault!"

It was sunny some day after my foray into the city in search of home. Omma was at the shack. She was readying herself for something. She did not eat. And she had us prepare to go out. We weren't dressed in our best but we were dressed nicer than we had in quite a while.

"Let's go." She hurried us out. She grabbed each of our hands and briskly led us down the hill. She clearly knew her way around. And this excursion was a first or at least a first since our fatherless residence at the shack on the hill. "How about I take us someplace nice?" she said looking ahead.

Here, then, my memory fails me again. I cannot find within me the seam that put this moment together with what I remember to be next. What I remember next was the blurry stream of building passing by through a window as the three of us were in the back seat of a taxi. The remarkable fact is that up to this point in my life, I may have been in a car just a couple of times, let alone a taxi, which was prohibitively expensive. And, looking back on my six year old self, I was much more aware of money, or the lack of it, than I can recall of any other six year old. The rarity of the episode made me nervous. There was the strange smell of the seat cloth and the people who sat in the very same place prior to our occupancy. Omma seemed nervous as well. She had not been inside of a taxi in a long time either. This is true, of course, if she had not ridden in taxis when she disappeared. My brother was... I think he was sleeping. Either way, he was playing yet another insignificant role in my memory.

My memories of Korea have very little of my brother. There are many reasons for this. My brother was a relatively happy and oblivious kid. He had these adorably sad eyes that no adult could resist. He was incredibly affectionate. He was very bright, though he still spoke with a child's senselessness. I do not know which caused which: did his looks and nature gain the attention of adults causing them to teach him more things early in life, or was he more of a learner than I was and therefore adults taught him things? Either way, his happy oblivious nature had him either on the sidelines, out of harm's way, away from conflict and protected by someone who paid close attention, or he was an accessory, held onto by the main characters of scenes as a cute prop, something to provide a little distraction when things got too heated. In either case, his presence never contributed to any change in the tides.

Not that I played a significant role in anything that happened, either. I was merely observing, always trying to pay attention to what was going on, trying to get my bearings and prepare myself. What I was preparing for is beyond me. But there never seemed to be a moment's rest, especially now that every little bit of information could help me get some much needed sustenance. And on that front, I had disregarded my brother's ability to contribute, never an active part of any episode of our Korean life.

We arrived at our destination. I was not sure where we were.

And my memory here has this trick. I recall getting out of the taxi on top of a hill, next to a donut shop. But later I recall looking out through the window of the same donut shop at a flat city scene.

Whatever the scene, the three of us, Omma, Soorin and I got out of the taxi and walked around a bit, I think. We were holding hands, I think. Omma was smiling, I think. I am not really remembering this "walking around." What I am really recalling is that Omma did not seem to know where we were going, though she seemed to have a destination in mind. And somehow we ended up back at the donut shop, back where we started, restarting this part of the plan. And there certainly seemed to be a plan.

It was not a fancy place, the donut shop, but I did recognize that the small shop had some seating next to the window and was successful enough to have an air of newness in that 1980s sort of way that most establishments in Korea did not.

Omma asked us to pick out what looked good.

Being in a donut shop is already exotic. Western food was expensive and donuts were no exception. Heightening the exoticism of the donuts on our plates, we were given western utensils. Soorin and I sat facing Omma. Omma was not having anything. She smiled and told us to enjoy it. And I did enjoy it. Soorin was clearly enjoying it.

For all the times I was envious of my brother being better looking, smarter and more popular, I still saw him as my little brother. I forced myself to learn to cook so he could eat. I dared myself to venture out into a world I did not know how to navigate so that we could see our father. And even when I sat on the sidelines, watching relatives play with him, often tickling his feet, I took pleasure in his laughs too. He had never caused me any pain. It was not really my little brother I was jealous of, although I had convinced myself of that then. It was everyone else I faulted for seeing through me. It was my fault for being so invisible. And, I feel, I must have known that somehow, even at six.

When I looked up at Omma, she was looking out of the window, far off some place, concerned. She was rubbing her middle finger with her thumb. That was where I held my pencils. That was where Omma held her *dambae* cigarettes. And as a reflex, she looked at Soorin and caught my eyes in the process, looking back at her. For a moment, she was a very pretty girl.

It was not long ago when she was hanging around my father's cafe in her school uniform, hanging out with her classmates waiting for him to park his motorcycle and walk in to do his session. My father was a popular DJ. In Korea, disc-jockeys who did not work at radio stations worked at cafes. There was a glassed-in booth setup with a turn table, a microphone and a shelf full of records, much like a radio station. The DJ introduced songs, talked about things that went on in the neighborhood and played requests for boys and girls who had the guts to stand at the booth in front of all of their classmates. DJ's were usually good looking, had good voices, and would often bring in a significant portion of a cafe's business during their sessions. And my mother hung around to exchange a word or two with the DJ, perhaps. And completely astounding her and her friends, she caught the eye of the DJ. Their innocent courtship did not last long. They were probably all of over each other in back alleys or behind the high school, like teenagers. Or at least that is how I imagine my parents before I came along.

186

My mother was a teenager, eighteen years old. She would have been in the middle of her senior year when she figured out that all the sneaking around had gotten her pregnant. She would have been able to graduate high school unscathed if she was carefully dressed since she probably did not show much, if at all, even during the final month of February. My parents were married April 30th. Strangely, the beautiful couple held their two week old son after the ceremony.

Omma still had eyes of a teenager; though the rest of her face was worn with the stresses of whatever it was that stressed her. Some of her classmates were only just getting married and there she was, twenty four, sitting across from her not one but two sons, the younger cute as a button and resembling her and the older being mini-Appa.

A very strange thing was taking place at the donut shop: we spent money on a taxi to go someplace we had never been before, I had an expensive western delicacy in my mouth, nearly jabbing myself with these metal things Americans jabbed their food with. And though she was smiling, it was off somehow. Riding a taxi was off. Eating donuts was off. Her face was tight, she was nervous. "I need to make a phone call."

The shop was small enough the middle-aged owner-lady behind the counter overheard and offered, "You can use our phone," she offered. This gesture was significant because each call had a cost.

"No, no. Thank you, but I couldn't do that. I will go out and make a call on the payphone (like everyone else)."

"Your little kids are right there. It's okay. I won't charge you for it."

"Really, I do not want to be a bother so…" Her back was facing us as she spoke with the lady. Even her back was tense. It may even have been shivering. She had her purse with her, her hand in it as though she was ready to take out some money for the payphone.

"It's no bother. Come on. It'll give me a chance to show off this thing."

"Thank you, but I will go to the payphone." With this, the lady gave Omma the 'suit yourself' look.

Omma had rejected the offer three times. She started to step back toward the door. She turned to me, or it seemed it was to me and not to Soorin. "I'm going to call a friend at the payphone. I won't be long. You be good. I'll be just right there." She fished for something in her purse, but pulled out her empty hand and closed it. "Challin-a, take care of Soorin."

Using the weight of her body, as though she had to exert great effort, she heaved the door open.

Then she ran away.

Her mane flew behind.

Contributors

FLIP THE SCRIPT: ADULT ADOPTEE ANTHOLOGY

TRACY AABEY-HAMMOND

TRACY AABEY-HAMMOND is a baby scoop era adoptee and adoptee rights activist. She writes about her experiences as an abused adoptee on her blog Adoptee Path. She has successfully entered reunion with the surviving members of her biological family in 2013. In addition to writing projects, she works as a business analyst in the insurance industry. Also a part-time college student, she devotes her remaining energy into her work as a metal-smith and jeweler. She is the owner of Tracy's Gem Shop on Etsy, and is widely known for her broken heart adoption pendants which are featured in this publication.

KEVIN MINH ALLEN

KEVIN MINH ALLEN was born Nguyễn Đức Minh on December 5, 1973 near Sài Gòn, Vietnam to a Vietnamese mother and American father who remain unknown to him. He was adopted by a couple from Rochester, NY and grew up in Webster, NY with his two younger sisters. In 2000, he moved to Seattle, WA to pursue a life less ordinary. Kevin is a poet and essayist who has had his essays and poetry published in numerous print and online publications, such as Eye To The Telescope, The International Examiner, and Northwest Asian Weekly. He had his first poetry chapbook published in July 2014, "My Proud Sacrifice." http://myproudsacrifice.tumblr.com/

LEIGHA BASINI

LEIGHA BASINI was born in Jeju, South Korea, adopted at seven months, and grew up in Charlotte, North Carolina. She published poetry and non-fiction in various journals and is now a healthcare attorney who writes things no one would want to read. She previously represented children in foster care. She is a graduate of Queens University, where she studied writing, French, and art, and Tulane Law School. She is a Francophile and loves politics, kimchi jigae, and traveling to far-flung corners of the world. She hopes to set foot on Antarctica and lives with her husband outside of Washington, DC.

MI OK SONG BRUINING

MI OK SONG BRUINING is a Korean adoptee, lived in NJ, RI, NYC, Boston and now lives and works in Providence, RI. She is a practicing licensed clinical social worker, accomplished artist, award-winning poet, and published writer. Mi Ok is grateful to be included in this anthology and her website is: http://www.mioksongbruining.com. She can be reached at miokbruining@gmail.com.

NICOLE J. BURTON

NICOLE J. BURTON is a playwright and author of twenty plays, a reunited adoptee from England, and author of *Swimming Up the Sun: A Memoir of Adoption.* She'll present her stage adaption of her book, *Swimming Up the Sun – The Play,* at next year's 2016 Capital Fringe Festival in Washington, D.C. It will also be filmed for live performance video distribution. Nicole lives in Riverdale Park, Maryland with her husband, photographer James Landry. Together they recently published *Memory Music,* a full-color book of photographs and found stories excerpted from James Landry's popular photo-blog, MusicFromTheFilm.blogspot.com, available through bookstores and on Amazon. Nicole@nicolejburton.com

ANNA CAVANAGH

ANNA CAVANAGH is a provisionally registered psychologist and PhD candidate in Clinical Psychology. She was born, adopted and raised in Germany and currently resides with her husband in Sydney, Australia. She started to come out of the adoption fog in 2014 and since then has been actively involved in the adoption community. She is interested in raising awareness of the challenges that adopted people can face and believes in creating positive change.

LARRY CLOW

LARRY CLOW is a writer, editor, teacher, and adoptee living in southern Maine. He's the editor of *The Sound,* a weekly newspaper, and is working on his first book, *People You May Know.*

ELIZABETH COLE

ELIZABETH COLE was adopted as an infant in 1974 in Minnesota. She grew up with loving parents and plenty of room to play. She used to sit in a tree in her back yard when she felt sad. At 18 Elizabeth gave birth to a baby boy who was placed for an open adoption with two of the most generous and kind people she has ever known. She has the privilege of having relationships with her birth mother's family and her son's family as well. She now lives in Madison, Wisconsin with her husband and two daughters.

LAURA COTTER

LAURA COTTER attends Bowdoin College in Maine. She enjoys mathematics, science, and art and hosts a weekly radio show dedicated to her favorite singer/songwriter, Taylor Swift. Laura was born in Jiujiang, Jiangxi, China. She was adopted when she was thirteen months old and grew up in Newton, MA. Laura would like to thank her sister Charlotte and her parents for their boundless support and dedicates this essay to the little boy, ChangMing, who helped her to find a connection to her own identity.

JOSHUA CROME

JOSHUA CROME is an adoptee born in Chicago, Illinois during the Baby Scoop Era. After four years of searching, he has been able to reunite with both sides of his natural family.

A #FlipTheScript re-tweeter and occasional poster, this is his first essay on the subject of adoption. Joshua is a magna cum laude graduate of Rider University, having majored in secondary education and history. He lives with his wife and children in New Jersey, and enjoys golf, cooking, and cars.

AMIRA ROSE DAVIS

AMIRA ROSE DAVIS is a black transracial adoptee who was born in Texas in 1988 and adopted as an infant and raised by two white mothers in Massachusetts. She has been reunited with her birth parents and siblings since 2009. Amira Rose is a Doctoral Candidate in History at Johns Hopkins University where she studies black women, sports and politics in the 20th century. She also teaches classes on black feminism, sports history, and race and media. Additionally, Amira Rose does public speaking events about adoption, teen/young pregnancy and parenting, and minority access to higher education. She is an Identity columnist at *Lost Daughters*. Amira Rose and her husband currently reside in Baltimore with their two children.

APRIL DINWOODIE

As Chief Executive of the Donaldson Adoption Institute, April Dinwoodie is committed to improving adoption laws, policies and practices through research, education and advocacy. April created a specialized mentoring program "Adoptment," in which adults who were adopted and/or spent time in foster care serve as mentors to youth in care and is a co-founder of Fostering Change for Children. As a trans-racially adopted person, April shares her experiences to help potential adoptive parents and professionals understand both the beauty and complexity of adopting children of another race.

MEI-MEI AKWAI ELLERMAN, PHD

MEI-MEI AKWAI ELLERMAN was born in NYC; adopted at 7 months. She lived in Europe until age 23. Harvard PhD in hand, she taught Italian literature and film for 30 years.

A scholar at the Brandeis Women's Studies Research Center, Mei-Mei is writing two memoirs: 1) on her decades-long search for her biological roots, 2) on her biracial adoptive mother's family history.

Fierce activist, as Director Emerita of Polaris, she is deeply committed to fighting human trafficking and adoption-related rights.

As Co-founder of the *AN-YA Project*, recent publications include contributions co-editing *Dear Wonderful You, Letters to Adopted & Fostered Youth*, and contributing to the anthology *Perpetual Child: Dismantling the Stereotype*. Mei-Mei also blogs on Chineseadoptee.com and is an avid photographer and Reiki master.

CECILIA HEIMEE FLUMÉ

CECILIA HEIMEE FLUMÉ 혜미 is an artist that was born in Pusan, S.Korea and grew up in a small village outside of Umeå, Northern Sweden. She is working mostly in watercolor and pencil with themes such as in-betweenship, adoption and the feeling of belonging, She takes great interest in postcolonial theory, class and gender studies. Cecilia is now studying her MA in Visual Communication at Konstfack, Stockholm.

For more artwork and contact, you can find her website www.ceciliaflume.se

SHANNON GIBNEY

SHANNON GIBNEY is a writer, educator, and activist in Minneapolis. Her Young Adult novel *See No Color* will be released by Carolrhoda Lab in November, 2015. Her writing has appeared in a variety of venues, including The Crisis, Gawker, and Inside Higher Ed. Gibney is Faculty in English at Minneapolis Community and Technical College (MCTC), where she teaches critical and creative writing, journalism, and African diasporic topics. A current McKnight Artist Fellow in Writing, and former Bush Artist Fellow, she lives with her husband and children in Minneapolis.

SARAH ELIZABETH GREER

SARAH ELIZABETH GREER is an actress, playwright, memoirist and solo performer living in New York City. She is a graduate of The William Esper Studio and holds a B.A. in Theater from Mount Holyoke College. A proud member of The Dramatist's Guild, she is currently working on a two-volume memoir inspired by The Eleusinian Mysteries and is in the process of creating a TV series based on her solo show. She can be reached at segreer80@aol.com

LYNN GRUBB

LYNN GRUBB is both an adoptee and adoptive parent. Lynn enjoys writing about the complexities of adoption and recently edited the adoption anthology, *The Adoptee Survival Guide: Adoptees Share Their Wisdom and Tools*. Lynn's other passions include genetic genealogy, reading non-fiction, watching true crime TV, and playing the keyboard and violin. Lynn blogs at *Lost Daughters* and *No Apologies for Being Me*.

JODI HAYWOOD

JODI HAYWOOD: born in the UK, raised in an international, closed relative adoption, reunited with both parents. Now married with a teenage daughter, Jodi is a contributor to the *Adoptee Survival Guide* and the *Adoption Therapy* series and author of the upcoming book *Attachment Unavailable?: Adoption, Autism and Attachment Disorder*. Currently working toward a psychology degree, she also writes fiction, runs marathons, and enjoys true-crime shows, vintage science fiction, and antique cars.

MEGGIN NAM HOLTZ

NAM HOLTZ (Nam) is a Korean adoptee working as an actress, artist and filmmaker in NYC. Nam attended New Trier High School in Winnetka, IL, and graduated cum laude from SUNY Purchase with a BFA in dance.

Nam has performed on Broadway and the West End in "The King & I". She has sung the music of Queen in "We Will Rock You" at Las Vegas' Paris, and toured across the USA in "Miss Saigon" and "Flower Drum Song."

Nam is currently producing a documentary film about adoption called, "Found in Korea," which was the catalyst for her poem "who cut my umbilical cord?" website: namholtz.com

SUSAN ITO

SUSAN ITO is a hapa adoptee and the author of the mini-memoir, *The Mouse Room*. She co-edited the anthology *A Ghost at Heart's Edge: Stories & Poems of Adoption*. She is a creative nonfiction editor at *Literary Mama*, and her work has appeared in *Growing Up Asian American, Choice, Hip Mama, The Bellevue Literary Review, Making More Waves* and elsewhere. She has performed her solo show, *The Ice Cream Gene*, around the United States. She writes and teaches at the San Francisco Writers' Grotto, at Bay Path University and Mills College. Her website is http://susanito.com.

SOOJUNG JO

SOOJUNG JO is the author of *Ghost of Sangju*, columnist at the *Lost Daughters* blog, and contributor to multiple anthologies. Soojung is an adoptee (Korea) and adoptive mother (China). She reunited with her first family in 2013. Soojung lives in Southern California with her husband and four children, who supply constant inspiration and entertainment.

CATHERINE A. JOHNSTON

CATHERINE A. JOHNSTON was adopted at eight days old during the height of the Baby Scoop Era. Hers was a closed, same-race adoption. She has been in (and out) of reunion with her birth/first mother for almost twenty years. Catherine is a fierce advocate for adoptee voices, adoption reform, feminism and social justice. Formerly a professional chef and now a part-time potter, she is a mother to an amazing eight-year-old transracial/transnational adoptee old who is confidently beginning her own journey.

MELISSA DAE SOOK KIM

During 4 years, Melissa Dae Sook Kim has transformed an 80 square meters space into an exhibition place, in the exhibition hall of La Louvière : "ART in the BOX" brought together local artists as well as artists from further areas.

The fingerprint that leaves traces is the subject she treats in several steps. The picture supposed to reflect reality gets modified or disappears totally using a process she has created and developed.

For the sake of truth, she leaves for South Korea when she is 30, hoping for a happy reunion. She had information about her biological mother. The missing piece of her file.

Her work has been displayed in Paris, Brussels, Barcelona, Dublin, and Seoul. Some are still abroad; some came back to la Louvière, where she lives close to her most beautiful creation, her son Alexis.

MILA C. KONOMOS

MILA C. KONOMOS was born in Seoul, South Korea in 1975, and adopted six months later into a White American family. In 2009, she reunited with her Korean mother and Korean father. Mila currently writes a column named after her retired blog, *Yoon's Blur*, at the collective writing project, *Lost Daughters*, in which she addresses and discusses the complexities of transracial and international adoption. She currently lives in Georgia with her husband and two children.

ADEL KSK

ADEL KSK, French artist born in Seoul, Graduated from EESAB of Rennes with the Honors, she began her art researches in multimedia performances, videos and installations around the themes of women transformations, childhood and identity.

She exhibited her work in China, Korea, Japan, North America and Europe « *Orientity, Oriental+Identity* » group and solo.

She now focuses her work in painting and ink drawings and takes part of another overseas artists group created in June 2015.

She lives in France and Belgium

www.adelksk.com

LUCY CHAU LAI-TUEN

LUCY SHEEN 周麗端 nom de plume Lucy Chau Lai-Tuen Made in Hong Kong. Exported to the UK as a transracial adoptee in the early 60s. Despite being dyslexic Lucy is actor, filmmaker, published author and poet. A produced playwright and has just completed two writing commissions; The Royal Court Theatre, London and a Nimble Fish writing bursary RePlay. Lucy's writing can be read in several anthologies *Perpetual Child: Adult Adoptee Anthology & Dear Wonderful You, Letters to Adopted & Fostered Youth* (The AN-YA Project). *Adoptionland: From Orphans to Activists* (Create Space). *Adoption Therapy* (Entourage Publishing). *The Adoptee Survival Guide: Adoptees Share Their Wisdom and Tools. The Dance Is New* (mardibooks). *Poeming Pigeons* (The Poetry Box).

WENDY M. LAYBOURN

WENDY MARIE LAYBOURN is currently a Doctoral Candidate in Sociology at the University of Maryland, College Park. At four months old, she was adopted into a military family who eventually settled in Memphis, TN. Experiences of racial division and bridge building have informed her perspective and academic work. Wendy's research interests focus on race/ethnicity and cross-racial bridging, examining them within socio-historic context with particular attention to racial ideology. She enjoys traveling, eating yummy food, and making notoriously long to do lists.

KATIE HAE LEO

KATIE HAE LEO is a writer and performer whose work has appeared in *Water-Stone Review*, *Kartika Review*, *Line Break*, and *Asian American Poetry & Writing*. Her chapbook *Attempts at Location* was a finalist for the Tupelo Press Snowbound Award and is available through Finishing Line Press. Her one-woman piece "N/A" premiered at Asian Arts Initiative in Philadelphia and was remounted at Dreamland Arts in St. Paul as part of *The Origin(s) Project*. Her produced plays include *Four Destinies* and adaptations of *Baseball Saved Us* and *A Single Shard*. For more on Katie, please visit www.katiehaeleo.com.

STEPHEN DAVID LUKESON

STEPHEN DAVID LUKESON (정은기) is a reunited adoptee, activist and radical lover of all people. He studied social work at Baylor University and international development at Eastern University's School of Leadership & Development. Stephen and his partner currently reside in New Haven, Connecticut.

JAMIE LYNN

JAMIE LYNN is a wife, mother of 3, and a chalk artist who enjoys spending time with family and friends. Art is where Jamie most easily finds her voice and processes the many aspects of her life including adoption. Her primary forms of strength and encouragement have come through her faith in God, support of a few very close people, and therapy. On her journey as an adoptee she has learned to see and accept the good, bad, grief, and loss in her adoption story. She is co-founder of an art group that offers support and encouragement to youth adoptees as they find their own voice and to learn to articulate their story including both the positive and negative aspects of what it feels like to be adopted.

M. C. MALTEMPO

M. C. MALTEMPO is an aspiring writer living in New York. He grew up in Seoul, South Korea until he was eight years old when he was adopted along with his blood brother. His mother is Chinese-American and his father is Italian-American. He grew up in Colorado until he moved east for college. He reconnected with his birth-father's siblings when he was twenty-five years old. He is currently working on a novel. Memory May Reveal is his debut.

KIMBERLY MCKEE, PHD

KIMBERLY MCKEE, PHD is an assistant professor in the Department of Liberal Studies at Grand Valley State University. Her research interrogates the institutional practice of international adoption in its examination of American adoptions of South Korean children. She received her Ph.D. in Women's, Gender, and Sexuality Studies from The Ohio State University. McKee serves as the Assistant Director of KAAN (the Korean American Adoptee Adoptive Family Network). She previously wrote for *Gazillion Voices* and is a current contributor to *The Lost Daughters*.

GRACE NEWTON

GRACE NEWTON is a student at Macalester College and a Chinese adoptee. She has interned for the company Land of Gazillion Adoptees LLC and served as editor for the college section of Gazillion Voices, the first adoptee led adoption magazine. Grace is a recent member of The Lost Daughters and is one of the founding members of her college's Transracial/Transnational Adoptee Identity Collective; both are places she has found a great sense of camaraderie. When Grace isn't discussing issues of race and adoption in person, she is writing about it online at her blog: redthreadbroken.wordpress.com

SUSAN HARRIS O'CONNOR, MSW

SUSAN HARRIS O'CONNOR, MSW is a national solo performance artist of her book *The Harris Narratives: An Introspective Study of a Transracial Adoptee*. Her narratives have been featured over 100 times at places such as the Harvard Medical School conference series, Smith College Summer Lecture series, NAACP and Starbucks Coffee. She is published by the Yale Journal of Law and Feminism and the esteemed journal, Adoption and Fostering where her racial identity theory for transracially adopted persons is featured. In 2014, she received the Outstanding Practitioner in Adoption Award from St. John's University.

KAYE PEARSE

KAYE PEARSE was adopted twice, both times in intra-family placements and was fortunate to have reunited with her mother and siblings. She now advocates for adoptee rights and is determined to have her own adoption annulled.

MSEd in hand, Kaye teaches middle school in Virginia. She was previously published in *Dear Wonderful You Letters to Adopted & Fostered Youth*. Her new children's book, *Wibber Dibber Doo*, will be available on Amazon in Fall, 2015.

Midst trees and solitude, Kaye spends her spare time playing music, gardening, beekeeping and caring for the various animals that share her life and acreage. Adoption-interrupted.blogspot.com

ZARA PHILLIPS

ZARA PHILLIPS, originally from the UK, is in reunion with her Birth Mother and half siblings. Author of *Mother me' an Adoptee's Journey to Motherhood.*(BAAF) Writer and performer of 'Beneath My Fathers Sky' Co writer with DMC "I'm Legit' and Director of a short doc 'Roots Unknown' Zara often facilitates workshops, writes and speaks on the topic of adoption. www.everythingzara.org

MATTHEW SALESSES

MATTHEW SALESSES was adopted from Korea. He is the author, most recently, of *The Hundred-Year Flood.* He has written about race and adoption for NPR, The New York Times, Salon, The Toast, the Center for Asian American Media, and many others. Follow him @salesses.

CHRISTINE SATORY

CHRISTINE SATORY is an associate professor of art at Ball State University. Adopted in 1958, she has only recently begun to address her life-long experiences as an adoptee in her artwork. Her current series, *Empty Vessels*, explores the impact of American social beliefs and Catholic religious beliefs on the development of an adopted child's identity. They are personal reflections of her childhood, her search for identity and her relationship with her adoptive mother. The artworks in this publication reflect her ongoing inner turmoil when confronted with American society's adoption myths.

LIZ SEMONS

LIZ SEMONS is a contributor to *Dear Wonderful, You Letters to Adopted and Fostered Youth.* She loves to write adoption songs. Liz truly hopes to lift the *Flip the Script: Adult Adoptee Anthology* and to help the adoption community fight for fostered & adoptee rights through her lyrics. *Dear Wonderful You* opened up a door for Liz to conduct a creative writing workshop with young adults who are a part of an Independent Living program. Many of the young adults have aged out of the foster system. She hopes to inspire and encourage the participants but also hopes to have fun and see a smile on their faces. You never know—they may just write a hit!

BEATA C. SKONECKI, LMSW

BEATA C. SKONECKI, LMSW is a reunited adoptee living with her partner, cat, and a lot of plants. She was born in Rzeszów, Poland, and adopted internationally as a baby. She earned a Bachelor's in Health and Human Services and a Master of Social Work from the University at Buffalo. Beata is deeply committed to fighting the stigma of chronic illness and disability, and in helping to create accessible living spaces for all. She serves on the Board of Directors for an international NGO, Glaucoma Eyes.

JOE SOLL 조 살, LCSW

JOE SOLL 조 살, LCSW Adoptee, Psychotherapist and Author of Adoption Healing... a path to recovery (paperback and kindle in English and German, and audio in English); Adoption Healing

Supplement; Adoption Healing Articles, etc. ; Adoption Healing... a path to recovery for mothers who lost children to adoption (paperback in English and Korean, kindle in English); I Almost Fell off the Top of the Empire State Building (autobiography); Boots Beaumont Mysteries: Evil Exchange, Fatal Flight and Perilous Passage. Facilitator of nightly internet chats and facilitator of Adoption Healing Weekends.

JULIE STROMBERG

Born, fostered, adopted and raised in Connecticut, Julie Stromberg reconnected with her natural parents and families in 1998. Since then, she has applied her lifelong experience as an adopted person to conducting critical analysis of global adoption practices. She holds a bachelor's degree in journalism from Loyola University Maryland and her essays on the adoption experience and industry have been published online and in print. In addition to advocating for adoption policy reform, she works as a copywriter and content strategist. She is currently pursuing a master's degree in user experience design. www.juliegmstromberg.com

ANNEGHEM WALL

ANNEGHEM WALL is a mother of 3 boys, a soon-to-be adoption researcher, mental health trainer and adopted person. She is passionate about prizing the experience of the individual and challenging stigma, particularly in relation to mental health.

Adopted through a private agency as a baby, and now in reunion (of sorts) with her birth mother, Anneghem is finding a place within the adoption community, blogging, creative writing, and working on a research proposal specifically concerned with the experiences of adopted people. She is a person centered therapist and works across statutory NHS and voluntary sector services in the field of trauma, based in Nottingham, UK. She also enjoys writing poetry, music festivals and swimming in the sea.

DARYN WATSON

DARYN WATSON is a reunited adoptee originally from Canada. His first reunion was with his birth mother and maternal family in 1995. Currently, he is a board member of Adoption Knowledge Affiliates (AKA) and a supporter of adoptee's rights for both children and adults. In recent years, Daryn has established contact with members of his paternal family.

Daryn earned a BA degree in Social Psychology from Park University in 2012. Daryn resides in Austin, TX with his wife Christine. His blog can be viewed at www.adoptionreunionrealities.wordpress.com.

DIANE WHEATON

DIANE WHEATON, a reunited adoptee, was born in Oakland, California. She is in reunion with her first mother and maternal first family. A mother to two grown children, a daughter and son, respectively, Diane lives in California with her husband and their two Alaskan Malamutes. Adopted as an infant in the closed adoption system, she began her search mid-life in a closed state. An advocate for open records and adoption reform, she is currently writing her first memoir and can be found blogging on adoption issues, family and life at dianewheaton.com.

CHRISTOPHER WILSON

The Director and producer of the documentary feature You Have His Eyes, Christopher Wilson's personal journey has now become the most highly accoladed film dealing with the subject of adoption on the market today. The directors first feature film has captivated audiences across America. Winning eight major awards in the preliminary stages of the film's festival circuit run. Including two best director nods, two audience choice awards, and two best of festival honors.

A South Florida native, Christopher is the founder and president of CTW Productions. He honed his film and writing skills while attending the private college, Hawaii Pacific University.

His entrepreneurial skills led him to become the CEO of 7one. A social organization intent on spreading an empowering message, "Live Life.7 days a week. One day at a time.", and positive lifestyle to the collective global community.

Editors

DIANE RENÉ CHRISTIAN (CO-EDITOR)

DIANE RENÉ CHRISTIAN founded the *AN-YA Project* in 2012, after publishing her debut novel, *An-Ya and Her Diary*.

As the founder of the *AN-YA Project*, Christian has edited/published— *An-Ya and her Diary: Reader & Parent Guide* as well as Co-edited/published *Perpetual Child: Adult Adoptee Anthology, Dismantling the Stereotype* and *Dear Wonderful You: Letters to Adopted & Fostered Youth*.

Flip the Script: Adult Adoptee Anthology is the fourth book Christian has edited and published under the *AN-YA Project* umbrella.

ROSITA GONZÁLEZ (CO-EDITOR & CONTRIBUTOR)

Adopted in 1968 at the age of one, Rosita Gonzàlez is a transracial, Korean-American, Holt International adoptee. Her road has been speckled with Puerto Rican and Appalachian relatives, including her perfectly-blended, multiracial sister, the natural child of her adoptive parents. While quite content with her role as a "Tennerican," her curiosity has grown recently as her children explore their own ethnic identities. She has discovered that her children, the second generation of adoptees, have inherited her racial ambivalence. As a result, Rosita has recently started her search for her natural family. With the help of G.O.A.'L., she visited Korea in August 2014 and fell in love with her birth country. When she is not supporting her children on their individual paths, Rosita spends her time as an art educator, ceramicist, art photographer and activist. She is passionate about issues of race, gender and adoption. She shares her adventures as an adoptee and parent on her blog, *mothermade*.

AMANDA H.L. TRANSUE WOOLSTON (CO-EDITOR)

AMANDA H.L. TRANSUE WOOLSTON is an author, speaker, and licensed social worker with a Bachelor's degree and a Master's degree in social work. Amanda has served the adoption and foster care communities through individual and family clinical work, group work, writing and presenting, and working for positive policy change. Her writing and presentations have reached broad audiences through multiple books, magazines, major news and radio interviews, and conferences, and she has engaged with legislators at the state and congressional levels on adoption policy. Amanda is probably best known for her personal blog, *The Declassified Adoptee*.

49606527R00111